disease. This is not to be misu
injuries that have yet to affect th
the aura before an illness starts to ~~rester of later to the physical~~
again proving that insight regarding your energy and aura is exceptionally
beneficial to all aspects of health and wellness (Martin, 2008).

It is always important to maintain or manifest a balanced mental aware-
ness and overall balanced wellness approach. We often do not realize how
much bad energy we conjure up inside ourselves by holding on to previous
damaging relationships. Whether they are physical or mental, or with an
object or a living being, we need to banish these kinds of relationships in
order to keep a healthy, balanced, vibrant, and all-around happy aura. It is
no secret that if you pursue something while in the right state of mind, then
the body will follow. Once your mind is manifesting good energy, then tran-
sitioning into your best self becomes easier (Martin, 2008).

You might find that energy pathogens (usually perceived as a disease
that thrives off your energy) come not only from your extended environment but also from your inner process. When we put out negative energy, it
is most likely to reflect back to us. Energy is a thing that flows, moves, and
adjusts. When two energies flow well together, it usually results in compatible auras that form a healthy bond. You can (and probably have or will)
encounter different auras that do not match up with your energy, and this
causes some chaos or turmoil in your life. Whether it comes from within or
from another source, this book will help you identify these compatible and
incompatible energies. It is also important to take note of the different
ways to avoid and banish these incompatible energy pathogens for you to
maintain a beautiful, vibrant aura that also acts as a reflection of the lovely
spirit that resides within you (Svirinskaya, 2015).

Biofields, or as we often call them, energy fields, can be somewhat
intimidating to study for some. It is a complex concept that takes even the
most gifted healers years to understand and grasp fully. It is not expected of
anyone to become an expert on biofields in order to live a life filled with
light. This book focuses more on learning the vibrational language of your
own biofield and adapting to it. The biofield is pretty much considered to
be the design of our existence. Its vibrational pulses are thought to be part
of the energy we manifest, and the light, often associated with colors, is
more simply described as our auras.

As stated before, our biofield (or energy field) can be damaged either by ourselves or by outer threats. It usually causes some sort of destruction or intrusion to our energy flow and creates a complete mess by contaminating or colliding with the balance of our energy and auras. Biofield therapies and balancing techniques will enable you to manifest, maintain, and protect your energy from various attributes like disease, malnutrition, toxins, parasites or pathogens, and mental distress. As mentioned previously, this will hopefully serve as your guide to protect your energy and your aura.

Surely, you know by now that everything you do has some sort of effect on you. These impacts can contribute to your energy's strength and wellness or they could become major bumps in the road. You cannot control everything that happens to you. However, it is important to have power over the things that you can control in order for you to demonstrate a healthy, balanced energy and aura. You deserve the life that this book is striving to help you build. You deserve a life filled with light, love, and balance.

Like pathogens, we may, at times, come across an energy vampire: a succubus that drains you emotionally, physically, and spiritually. These are often very seductive and attractive beings, and it is hard to detect their draining nature from the get-go. There is certainly not a person alive who has not encountered one of these people. We can also be energy vampires ourselves without completely noticing it from time to time. That is why it is so important to always reflect inwards, as well. Finding our weak moments or emotions and dealing with them head-on will add to our journey of light and healing.

During your time here, you will be given an in-depth look at energy vampires and how they function or enable themselves to manipulate, control, and drain us. This will enable you, as the reader, to set boundaries and take control of your own power and energy. Protecting your energy will solve most of the problems that energy vampires can conjure up. In order to be firm and stable, it is important to gain confidence and resilience during this epic journey. You definitely have it in you; you just have to locate the access key first.

This metaphorical access key will also help you live your own truth. The media can have such a hold on us mentally and spiritually. Not only does it tell us what to buy, how to be, and what to eat, it also drains us and keeps us shackled to their approval and guidance. This book aims to teach you how to perceive or consume media without succumbing to its mental slavery.

We tend to forget how ritualistic we are as humans, or we simply just don't notice it. Rituals can be fulfilling and helpful. Forming balanced habits that add to your energy and the vibrancy of your aura can be beneficial in many ways. This is not just another how-to guide on living a healthy life-style; it is insightful information to help you live your best life, which is what you deserve.

Ultimately, we want to be able to protect ourselves and live a life filled with positive vibrations. In order to do that, it is often necessary to deflect another's energy away from yourself and back onto them. Projecting posi-tive vibrations will lead to positive vibrations being projected onto you, and the same goes for toxicity.

This book will be your easy access sensei, teaching you energy defense tactics that will help you fight off negative auras, vibrations, and energy by deflecting it back onto the receiver and avoiding any contamination.

Meditation is a crucial part of opening up your aura to light and love. Working this into your list of rituals will offer you clarity, healing, and a moment for positive reflection. It will also nourish your energy and create space for a more positive energetic flow to enter your space.

Healthy auras tend to result in healthy energy. Throughout this book, this concept will be constant. The reason it comes up so frequently is because we all need to be reminded from time to time that we do deserve a life filled with love and light. This is a journey, not a sprint; it is important to take time to reflect upon and live your life. This book will be here when you need it, and it will still be here when you do not. Hopefully, by the end of it, you will become (and feel) fully equipped to take ownership of your energy and aura, as well as become its protector. If you have already started your journey, then this book will be your new best friend and support system throughout each and every endeavor.

YOU are a unique aura that produces unique energy which is expressed in this universe. Throughout your life, you will face many experiences and meet various people that will bring you light, joy, love, and fulfillment. You will also go through many hardships and have times when it will be hard for you to remain positive. However, you will survive and thrive because this book will enable and empower you to have ownership of your true self and protect your own, precious energy.

It is not an easy journey, but it is a beautiful one - even if the road can sometimes become riddled with darkness. Remember, though: you have already gathered the strength to radiate your love and light over this path, and that always takes some courage. This book will help you become the light source for others when they need it, but it will also teach you to avoid drowning yourself in your own efforts. Also, it will enable you to love those who need it without losing too much love for yourself.

This book is not only your insight into a world of enlightenment, but also a book about goodness and manifesting positivity within yourself. You are a unique life force, and you have the capability to live a fulfilled life. You will feel these forces come back to you in abundance, and you will be able to protect your energy and project positive vibrations.

UNLOCKING THE MAJESTY OF YOUR ENERGY

ENERGY FIELDS AND AURAS

When you look at the study of physics, you will find that the fundamental concept of energy is based upon the science of a physical, or literal, body of methods performing the task of physical or actual work. According to Krieg (Carroll, 2015), energy is the technical term used to describe the power to move things, either prospective or tangible. He also claims that energy is not of its own existence, but rather an attribute or feature of something. In physics, you get various types of energy like kinetic, thermal, and chemical energy.

The energy we discuss throughout this book probably has some sort of link to the study of physics. However, luckily, we will not be needing a physics lesson for this journey. We will be focusing on a more spiritual approach to energy, especially the steps you can take to protect your energy and how to curate positive vibrations using it.

All living organisms, including humans, possess unique signifiers that give us life. The belief system around vitalism is an ancient one and is still prevalent in our modern world. Not everyone shares the same opinion about it and, unfortunately, not everyone basks in its glory. The existence of this force has many names because it has been explored in many cultures worldwide.

The most common cultural participants are Hindu, Chinese, and Japanese. Prana, qi/chi, and ki are the words often used to describe or identify the source of life that is body, mind, and soul (Stenger, 1999). It is also referred to as orgone energy by some. Although it has different names amongst various people, it is important to remember that the meaning you prescribe to it is the most important. You can call it whatever you want - it is still YOURS.

If we were to strip down the anatomy of our physical bodies, we would discover atoms. Everything that exists in this world is made up of them. Now, it is important to remember that these atoms are filled with emptiness. It might sound weird, but this is mainly because everything in this world is made up of energy and not matter. (Svirinskaya, 2019).

In order to grasp this concept at first, you should refrain from pitting physics and the concept of energy fields against each other. One should remain open to exploring different ideas and arguments surrounding energy and auras. If you do, however, feel conflicted, feel free to carry on reading. Once you have completed each chapter of this book, you will have a better understanding of this concept and be able to resolve any conflicting thoughts.

Energy comes in waves, and we, as energy-beings, can emit and submit to these waves. There can be various waves occurring around us at a single time, vibrating at certain frequencies. The atoms that make up our physical bodies are constantly generating energy waves and, therefore, vibrations at a frequency. This helps conceptualize that we are not made up of solid matter but rather atoms in motion.

It is definitely strange to perceive ourselves as a bunch of atoms constantly bustling about, so it is fine to feel overwhelmed with grasping this concept. It is important that you come to terms with it, though, before continuing this journey. Being content with your physical existence is one of the starting points.

This energy your body produces creates a field around your physical body, which is what we refer to as our aura. Your aura is the manifestation of both your physical and spiritual bodies. One can even refer to it as the light of your existence reflecting your state of being. As we radiate, a certain frequency or amount of energy extends around our body, usually moving up from the ground and from above coming down on us. These forces are known as terrestrial (coming from the ground) and universal (coming down from above) (Svirinskaya, 2019).

Your energy exists or can be viewed in seven different layers forming around your body. These layers cooperate and communicate with one another to convey signals regarding your body, mind, and spirit, whether it is health, emotions, pain, etc. They can also communicate several signals or forces at once.

The forces mentioned above can also communicate with those of another person. Surely, you have heard of the term *vibes*. This word is usually a simplified way to express the concept of vibrational frequencies. Your aura is pretty much made up of these vibrations. The energy we put out has the amazing ability to communicate with others what its/your current state may be. For example, when someone is physically ill, we can easily sense that they have low energy, or when you are in a room filled with people, you may sense certain emotions being emitted from someone else. This is usually their energy telling others what they are experiencing without them uttering a single word.

Another famous figure of speech that is often used is *your vibe attracts your tribe*. This saying exists because we can often sense each other's auras, and that can either cause tension or comfort. Surely, there are a lot more complex outcomes or feelings that could come from vibrational frequencies, but we will discuss more of that in the chapters to follow.

Almost every time you catch a glimpse of an auric illustration, you will notice that the aura is drawn away from the body and is not attached to the physical body. It usually seems like some sort of armor or shield instead of a part of us. It is highly advised not to focus too much on such illustrations. We are almost kind of embossed into our auras. It is often referred to as an "auric-egg", as stated earlier. This is a great way to understand how we sit in our auras.

Imagine a whole egg, not even slightly cracked. When you consider the contents of the egg (the white and the yolk), you can grasp that there is no space between the shell and its contents. In this case, our physical bodies are the yolks and our auras the white and shell parts. We are one hundred percent drenched in our auras, with no gaps in between. (This imagery is often found in Kirlian photography, which is a method used to capture the essence of one's aura in a visual or photographic way.)

Every single person has a unique aura. They can be similar to another's but never the same. It is as unique as a fingerprint, if not more distinctive. Yes, our auras may be compatible with some more than others, but think of it this way: just because you have a few things in common with someone does not mean you are the same person. Your vibrations may complement someone else's and vice versa, but it can never be identical. Please remember that our auras can never be "hidden" or "turned-off". Also, the vibrancy of our auras may be equal, but the waves of energy we send out always differentiate from one another's, even in the smallest ways.

According to Sarah A. Schweitzer (2013), our auras act as decipherable collectors for our collective body. Because of our general special qualities, we will display, submit, and interact with the stimuli of other people's auras and all their external waves and frequencies in our own distinctive way. We cannot react identically when our auras are stimulated or responsive. This alone proves that each person's aura is uniquely wired to comprehend existence in its own way. The fact that we are all collectively experiencing this uniqueness goes to show how majestic unity can be between different auras omitting various vibrations.

Another interesting demonstration of how our auras react in a unique way is to think of when someone with a contagious sickness enters a room and only contaminates some of the surfaces, but not all of them. Only some of the people catch the virus or sickness, but not all of them. This is because some auras will accept a virus, and some will deflect it, proving our previous analogy.

It is also important to understand that our auras are not capable of controlling us. It is a gathering of our identity, frequencies, wellness, behavior, mental and physical health, and many other things. It is impossible for our auras to make us act a certain way, as they cannot act independently from us and use some weird form of mind control to use us as their puppets. Our auras merely answer to our energy frequency contributions.

When your aura is affected by someone else's negative energy, it does not subconsciously make you slap that person. It simply behaves as a receiver and a correspondent of the incoming vibrations that are entering your auric space. This does not exactly mean that seeing or anticipating someone else's aura is going to be a natural action for you.

When we are attempting to access our own auras, if we can hone in on certain aspects and concentrate hard enough on particular things, we are also more aware and familiar with ourselves and our bodies, minds, and spirits. Thus, we can analyze our own auras more effectively than someone else's. We have no control over other people's thoughts, actions, feelings, and health. Because each aura is so unique and diverse, it takes someone who is trained in reading auras to perform an accurate analysis of someone's energy field. However, there are rare instances where someone's aura is extremely vivid, thus making certain aspects of it easy for the untrained eye to sense (Schweitzer, 2013).

When it comes to the colors that are often associated with our auras, we should be careful. Colors concerning our energy and associated with other sensory information does not always coincide. For example, we know that the color red can be symbolic of love and danger. When it comes to your aura, the color red could suggest you are stable, dominant, strong, and/or determined, amongst many other things. Auras and color will, however, be presented in the final chapter of this book.

TAKING OWNERSHIP OF YOUR ENERGY

A lot of negative entities can enter your aura if you do not take the time to study and assess your own energy. What is visible to the untrained or naked eye is not necessarily an indication or evidence of your existence or your being. The common mistake we often make is to think of ourselves as physical beings who are just taking up space instead of viewing ourselves as the spiritual creatures that we truly are.

As previously mentioned, we are made up of atoms that are constantly moving and creating vibrating frequencies. The physical body is merely a vessel that our mind and spirit occupy. If you struggle to grasp this concept, take the time to reflect on the idea that our auras are a dwelling master of our physical, mindful, and spiritual existence.

As it goes, one should always keep in mind that we must not only focus on our physical well-being in order to improve our lives. As we already know, each aura is unique, and our energy has its own identity. It is important to be fully aware of every aspect of yourself. The clearer your idea is about yourself, the clearer your aura and the identity of your energy will become. Being your true self is crucial when you are pursuing positivity and wellness. This task can never truly be fulfilled, because circumstances, feelings, health, and other aspects of our lives are constantly changing. This is inevitable. Becoming familiar with your authenticity will give you a concrete understanding of how your energy flows and the way your aura receives and sends out vibrations.

This knowledge about yourself can often be difficult to comprehend and not the most pleasant information to work from, but discovering your authenticity can help you shift your attention to the parts that you need to heal or work on. Someone who does not know themselves often will not realize how easily chaotic energy can enter their aura and how badly it can affect their mind, body, and spirit.

Unfamiliarity and unawareness of your true self is dangerous and unhealthy. Your aura can become cluttered with the wrong energy and submit to or become intruded by various threats. This will stand in the way of your balance, and you will inevitably attract the wrong people, which is usually how energy pathogens and vampires grab a hold of us and bleed us dry. There will be more in-depth discussions on these concepts as we move along.

With time, you will learn that when an aura is dull or radiates and receives too much negative energy, it can become quite small, confined, and/or shrunken. This is because your aura tends to tighten itself in a sense so as to protect and sustain the physical body during times of trouble or illness. Please do remember that if you receive an aura reading and the results of it reflect something that may not sit well with you, it does not mean that this will be a constant. It is crucial to consider your circumstances at the time of the reading. We do not always have control over the things that happen in our lives, and if you are hard on yourself unnecessarily, you will damage your aura all on your own.

It is often helpful to think of your aura as a force of nature like a tree, for example. When a tree receives nourishment and light, it grows big and sprouts beautiful flowers and luscious leaves. When it is deprived, butchered, or infected with pests/parasites, it does not grow as beautifully and eventually dies out if no rescue attempt is made. Similar to this metaphorical tree, we also need nourishment, light, and positive vibrations in order to grow and live contentedly. All living things have this need. Your physical body, your mind, and your soul all need various types of nourishment in order to maintain a vibrant, vivacious, and expansive aura.

Owning your distinctive energy and creating a balanced aura is not an easy task at all. It is important to remember that your feelings are valid, and they demand to be confronted. Your energy cannot lie, and whether you send off harsh distraught vibrations or pulsating positive ones, it does become noticeable. People who know you well or who bond with you occasionally can often feel your energy and the physical, mental, or spiritual vibrations that it is giving off. Complete strangers can even feel or notice if your auric field is large and your vibrations become prominent, whether they are positive or negative.

Everything we think is also energy, as is anything verbally uttered. It is vital to immediately release and recycle negativity. Owning your energy and aura means taking responsibility for the thoughts you allow yourself to have. Letting go of these self-sabotaging thoughts is not easy for anyone, but surely, you will feel lighter once you learn how to remove negative attachments.

You can either use them as lessons, taking only the parts from it that led to improvement, or you can recycle it into something completely new and different from its previous state. With self-sabotage, for example, you can entomb these negative thoughts. They will not go away instantly, but recycling our negative thoughts into positive ones or using critical thinking can improve our mental and spiritual energy.

Energy attachment is also more widely known as negative vibrations. Every time we take something away, we must put something back to ensure that we do not create a void or a potential opening for more negative vibrations or attachments. Naturally, we deal with any negative attachments by cutting them off like we would remove a cancerous organ from our physical bodies. You can do that by visually conjuring up that attachment in your mind and then switching it to something that makes you calm and content, like a "happy place" or "safe space".

By teaching yourself how to switch between these two contrasting thoughts or energies, you will find that it becomes more controllable over time. This will eventually lead to you gaining full control over the vibrations you are sending out or receiving from others, which ultimately means you will gain more and more ownership over your aura and energy.

Another thing to bear in mind is that you can also be a negative attachment to others, not only yourself. When you constantly refuse to look inward and reflect on the harm or pain you have inflicted upon others, you never are able to own your energy. Ownership requires accountability, responsibility, and a willingness to improve or heal the parts of yourself that are sending out these negative vibrations. Even if you are doing something like thinking badly about others, this energy becomes toxic and leaves a crippling effect on your aura.

As mentioned previously, energy does not lie, and intoxicating your own aura and someone else's (projecting these negative vibrations out onto others verbally or mentally) will immediately unhinge your vitality. So, not only does it terrorize your energy but the energy of others, too. Someone who owns their energy knows how to bury and recycle this negativity. The better we become at banishing or recycling negative attachments, the more control we gain over ourselves and our lives.

This does not necessarily mean you have to apologize to everyone you have ever wronged, but it does, however, mean you should take responsibility for your actions. You are also not obligated to "hash it out" with someone who has wronged you or who demands an apology. Nor are you obligated to accept an apology. Quite frankly, this has nothing to do with anyone else but YOU. You need to heal yourself. By healing and growing, you will find it easier to forgive and let go of the things that weigh you down or affect your wellness in a detrimental way.

In the next chapter, we will discuss toxic energy that you may come across in your environment and its surrounding influences, which will also give you an understanding of outward attachments that can harm your energy and aura.

2

TOXIC ENERGY

TOXIC ENERGY AND SURROUNDING INFLUENCES

S omething that we pick up quite early on in our journey is that energy recedes and surges. This means it has the ability to create an ebb and flow movement. Outside influences (or as we refer to them, surrounding influences) can noticeably impact the current or long-lined condition of our energy. Energy can multiply and divide, which can result in energy fluctuations from time to time. This counts for positive and negative energy alike. Understanding that both neutral and toxic energy is transmittable will open up different possibilities and capabilities to aid us in protecting our unique auras and owning our energy.

The more optimistic we are spiritually, the easier it becomes for positive energy to settle and stay, which helps our mind, body, and spirit remain in a positive state. Before we get too comfortable with this concept, it is important to note that the same goes for toxic or bad energy.

This is a true indicator of importance when it comes to protecting our own energy from outside threats. Being fully aware of these entities, from their power to their approaches, will enable us to refrain from being exposed to the darkness that they can instill upon our lives on Earth.

This chapter will inform you of toxic energy and its capabilities. We will also take a look at some of the surrounding influences that generate toxic energy and glance at a few of its various forms.

Toxic energy, like any other form of energy, comes in many kinds and from many circumstances. Toxic energy can affect all aspects of your physical body, mind, and spirit. If you imagine the idea of toxicity, it is convenient to come at it with an approach that is more linked to the idea of deliberately feeding yourself something toxic or poisonous.

We can turn towards indulging in toxic substances from time to time, and we can also be toxic entities, whether it is conscious or subconscious. This chapter focuses on this energy and collective consciousness and how it infiltrates our auras.

The easiest way to identify a toxic entity is to look at the key signifiers, or aspects, that point to toxicity and reflect on how this certain energy made you feel or react towards it or in its presence. It is also important to remember that all aspects or characterizations of this entity might not match up to full-on toxicity, but the toxic energy that it/they is submitting towards your space might not be compatible or may even be harmful to your wellness. Toxic energy not only comes from physical human beings, but it can also be linked to environmental, natural, and social energies.

Let's look at some of the signifiers that can make it easier for us to comprehend what toxic energy is.

The first thing we notice about a toxic energy is the chaos it seeds into our lives. For example, when a toxic person enters your space, you will not necessarily notice or succumb to their toxic nature right away. As the relationship or as their occupancy in your space grows, your life will start to feel less natural and more chaotic. It is normal for new relationships to change our circumstances, routines, or habits, but it can be detrimental to your aura's balance if this energy is toxic.

Remember: energy can be anything that causes vibrations and waves. Chaos can be exciting if it is healthy, but that is never the case with toxic energy. If it makes you feel deranged, unhinged, and scattered, then it is most likely toxic. Do not blame yourself if you totally misjudged this concept at first; toxic energies can manipulate their form into something disguised as attractive or pure.

Toxic energy also has a tendency to influence our moods and how we treat others. If you feel like you have been a bit more on edge and reacting more hostile towards others (yes, even objects), then there might be some toxicity brewing somewhere. Ending relationships or bonds suddenly is often a sign of sudden detachment, which means this toxic force is controlling or even manipulating the vibrations you are releasing into the world and the small space in your mind that enables you to snap out of it.

When we personify toxic energy, arrogance is one of the adjectives we use that is a clear indicator of the nature of this energy. Toxic energy deems itself enhanced. It sees no flaws in itself and cannot experience any form of ego death. This can make you believe that you are deficient, even though you are not. Surely, confidence is an important vibration to give off if it is purely intentioned. However, the condescension that exists in toxic energy is usually shameless. It flaunts, brags, and behaves pompously in order to inflict a sense of inferiority amongst other beings. This toxic energy is usually more prevalent in humans than other beings.

Whether it comes in the form of a thought, a random object, animal, or person, it has the ability to consume most of your energy and other aspects of your life. It separates you from your own life and the control you have over it. It also consumes most of your physical, mental, and spiritual capacity, which further escalates into more and more negative energy being exchanged back and forth.

It is safe to say that if negative energy becomes an all-consuming thing in your life, it is highly toxic. It separates you from your vitality and eventually becomes a great burden that can even affect day-to-day, mundane tasks. Although it has the potential to deprive you of certain vibrations, it is important to remember how strong and resilient you are and what a capable being you are.

By now, we know that toxic energy comes in many forms and shapes. Dark spirits and entities can collide with and latch onto our physical bodies and auras. This disturbs the way we think, speak, and act, and it also affects our desires and feelings. The entity that is possessed or occupied by these gloomy little pests often takes on the attributes, diseases, and overall behavior of the spirit or entity. Many times, this causes a shift in the person/entity's disposition.

Another form of toxic energy is through the power of thought. They are usually linked to feelings of hatred, envy, and jealousy and are the conjuring result of underlying negativity towards someone or something. They can cling to basically any layer of our auras and be the reason for various physical, emotional, mental, social, and spiritual instabilities and irregularities.

Previously, we mentioned that owning your energy and aura is extremely important, and taking responsibility for the energy you put out in the world has to be in place for this to happen. Every being is capable of attracting negative/toxic energy to themselves. This can occur without the contribution of outside sources, which we will discuss further later in this chapter. This happens most often when we react to fear for an excessive amount of time - longer than the aura can handle. This does not necessarily occur during moments of abrupt floods of a certain feeling or emotion. This negative feeling, experience, emotion, or thought has to fester in order to pollinate your aura with toxic energy.

Toxic energy also penetrates the aura when we participate in destructive habits, such as the use of harmful substances. When we are under the influence of a dangerous substance, our auras can be vulnerable to invasive toxicity. (These substances, depending on what they are and what they do, can still be used in moderation or in a controlled and safe environment.) Violence and tension can also open up your aura to threatening energy because of its negative nature.

Toxic energy has devastating effects on the aura. As we now know, toxic energy can be presented to us in many forms. Whether it takes the shape of negative thoughts, habits, or people, toxic energy and negativity do not just appear out of the blue. In this world, we find that anything that generates energy reacts to or creates certain environments.

These conditions or environments then surround our auras and influence our energy. It is, therefore, safe to assume that your surroundings can generate toxic energy by influencing the environment. In order to protect our auras from these influential surroundings, we must be able to identify its damaging attributes and learn how to deal with them, which will be discussed further on.

There are so many different surrounding influences that can elevate toxic energy and aid in its will to enter our auras. Unfortunately, there is not enough time in a day nor enough pages in this book for us to go over each and every one in detail. For the sake of our journey, we will touch on those that we encounter most in our daily lives and that hold a certain significance to our current modern lives. These influences can come from social, environmental, physical, or mental entities. This means that they can make up quite a list, as you probably can imagine.

If these surrounding influences are not applicable to your life, try switching them out with ones that you can relate to more realistically. This will also be a great way to exercise an independent interpretation of the knowledge we give you - one that better suits your unique situation. After all, YOU are the significant being that decided, admirably, to take ownership of your life.

The first surrounding influence we will be discussing is pollution. By no means are we listing these according to their prevalence or in this order for any other specific reason. You are unique, and thus, your aura will react to these surroundings in a unique way. Pollution, especially air pollution, has dire effects on our physical health. As mentioned before, our physical, spiritual, and mental existence is attached to our aura and can affect each aspect and layer of this energy field.

According to the Barcelona Institute for Global Health (ISGlobal), air pollution is directly linked to the causes of some of the worst respiratory diseases around. Some of them include lung cancer, strokes, and emphysema, among many others. The effects these diseases have, not only on our physical bodies but on our energy, is quite scary. When the physical body becomes ill (especially extremely ill), the aura shrinks, and its vibrancy fades to a dull tone. Our energy frequencies also pulsate less vigorously.

This is because diseases, especially potentially fatal ones, make the aura work even harder to protect itself against other invasive energies. Breathing is obviously a necessity to stay alive, but it is also an enormously important part of various healing therapies, rituals, and exercises. Pollution of any sort can overwhelm the aura and energy frequencies. In order to protect our energy, we must be vigilant of the toxic energy that pollution can create (Ranzani et al., 2020).

People - even those we love and adore - can also be contributors to toxic energy. This might come as no surprise, seeing that humans can be quite toxic due to their own shortcomings or auric troubles. As a side note, please keep in mind that it is important for us to approach even the most toxic entity with love and light in order for our own auric health to remain stable. When we find ourselves exchanging vibrations with other people or sharing a space with someone, it can often become toxic.

Being aware of another person's ability to contaminate your aura with toxic energy is never easy, because human relationships, communication, and interactions are quite complex as it is. An example of this could be a toxic work environment or relationship. When sharing a space with someone drains you or makes you feel anything but content, it is considered a surrounding influence for toxic energy.

Your own behavior towards others and yourself is also a surrounding influence that invites toxic energy into your aura. Earlier in this chapter, we learned that your own actions, thoughts, and energy can attract toxic energy. Acknowledging your own toxic behavior is a form of healing and a step towards enlightenment. Feeding your low self-esteem and being envious towards another or acting unlovingly towards another entity, for example, only attracts more negative energy. Creating a space for toxic energy to fester in will not end well for anyone or anything that is pursuing an enriched life on this earth.

Objects are also potential harbors of toxic energy. They can become significant to us because they can be aesthetically pleasing, sentimental, useful, or meaningful. Whether we can see it or not, objects also radiate vibrations and, as we now know, they also have energy. We all have something that binds us to a loved one or reminds us of a pleasant memory.

There does not necessarily have to be a concrete reasoning or explanation behind your attachment to this energy, but we often regard objects as harmless because they are not living entities that can react towards us physically. However, because objects carry energy, there is the possibility that they can carry toxic energy. It is extremely hard to read energy off an object, but many healers are capable of it. Once again, there is no certain way of knowing except by listening to your inner self or checking the signs.

Let us use an example to clarify this concept: if we receive an object from someone and put it in our space, their energy can be transferred through it, or the object can absorb the toxic energy from that someone. When this object is occupying your space, you are unintentionally creating an opportunity for that energy to infiltrate your aura. Ultimately, we should make an effort to find clarity regarding the objects we surround ourselves with, especially if it was something given to you by someone who is not necessarily your biggest fan.

Objects are also known for absorbing the energy of those who have left their physical bodies on Earth (those who have passed away). These items can still send out the vibrations that they have collected from the deceased. This can be toxic, but in contrast, it can also be comforting energy from time to time.

These next few chapters of the book might be a bit of a downer, but if we do not discuss the possible threats and challenges to protecting our auras and owning our energy, it can lead to ignorance and confusion. Ignoring the scary parts of this journey is like entering an exam without studying. When we are ill-prepared for what is to come, it can often lead to failure (or, in this case, an unhealthy aura that sends out stale vibrations and/or chaotic energy).

These chapters will equip you with the necessary knowledge to start your journey safely and with vigilance. Energies stay or hover where we "left" them, and it is important to know how to remove them when they become detrimental to our wellness. Cumulative toxic energy can clutter your aura and overwhelm your entire existence or being, which can have a very significantly destructive outcome.

You are a precious entity, and the purpose of this book is to teach you how to protect yourself and live a magnificent life. This does not necessarily mean that you will inevitably encounter these things, but considering every possibility is a sure-fire way to prevent you from losing progress or feeling ambushed.

Feel free to view this book as a well-lit torch that will guide you through the corridors of your body, mind, and spirit. It is important to take this seriously and refrain from tampering or colliding too much with potential dangers to your aura. You are a unique and purposeful entity who deserves the ableness and willingness to protect your energy.

✥ 3 ✥
ENERGY VAMPIRES

ENERGY VAMPIRES DEFINED

The term "energy vampire" is pretty self-explanatory. These entities present themselves in various spaces of our lives and often come disguised as loving, charismatic, or trustworthy beings. They do not look like the fictional vampire characters we often see in movies or read about in books. It is a blanket term or metaphor for someone who feeds off of your energy and eventually leaves you drained and your aura almost totally dull. They are also not associated with the subculture that attracts people who physically drink the blood of others or have any ties to the occult. To be clear, they are called "energy vampires" because of their ability to drain us of our energy.

It might be an odd concept to familiarize yourself with, but this chapter will explain the significance of identifying them and protecting your energy and aura from their narcissistic nature. It is absolutely possible to become impervious to their power. If you have ever felt relief or like a weight has been lifted off your shoulders when someone leaves your space, then it is most likely because that person or entity was, in fact, some form of (or even a full-on) energy vampire.

When you enter an area and almost immediately feel like your energy is decreasing, it can be indicative that one is near or approaching you. It can also be apparent that someone/something is a draining force when you feel the need to make up excuses for almost anything. You will most likely feel like your light is dimming and often struggle to find the reasoning behind it. When you reflect on your energy and cannot find any signs of self-inflicted drainage, it can also be because you are about to encounter a demanding, draining, and forceful entity.

When someone's presence is either intimidating or feels somewhat intrusive, you will immediately notice a variety of different vibrations coming from your own aura and theirs. Similar to toxic energy, it can take some time to realize what exactly is happening. Our human nature often forces us to search for flaws in ourselves before we even consider that an outside entity might be the problem. When we cannot find an explanation or a result that is located from within, it is most likely coming from outside of ourselves.

It is also very prevalent in instances where we feel like we would rather inconvenience ourselves in order to avoid an encounter than actually face the person or entity. When you sense your body is entering a fight or flight mode, it is important to validate that feeling, because it can be an attempt to warn you of a possible threat or, in this case, an energy vampire. Most of us feel physically sick before or during an encounter with one. Queasiness, sudden fatigue, stress, and other signs can be a result of another underlying issue. That is why it is important to educate yourself on the concept of energy vampires so that you do not become confused and focus your energy on the wrong intruder, surrounding influence, or ailment.

Your aura can also become trapped. One physical indicator of this is when you struggle to breathe when that energy enters your space, or even if you just think of a possible encounter with an energy vampire. You will almost become claustrophobic, even if you are not in a confined space, such as amongst a very large crowd. This irrational fear of becoming trapped or not finding an escape can be very overwhelming. Once you become vulnerable, it can make it easier for that entity to hone in on you and feed on your energy, leaving you dried out and dull.

Energy vampires are demanding beings that keep wanting more and more. They are not easily satiated and can often leave us feeling bad about ourselves and extremely exhausted. They consume our energy, because they are spiritually and mentally weak and, therefore, unable to create their own energy.

According to the American School of Hypnosis (American School of Hypnosis, 2015, 03:15–05:21), there are different types of energy vampires. The first one we will be discussing is the "victim". They tend to lack the ability to take responsibility for their own energy, and they always have an excuse, even when they are fully equipped to help themselves. When we open ourselves up to their tendencies, they can chip away at our energy.

Another type of energy vampire is called "the downer". These are the ones who simply find negativity in every certain thing or place. There can be a million waves of positive energy flowing their way, and they will still only focus on the one negative thing. They always have a tendency to create a negative atmosphere and have a high disregard for positive entities. Yes, it is normal to be aware of negativity at all times, but these energy vampires seek it out and thrive off it. It can become exhausting for a positive being to be around someone who is that conflicted and who drains the life and light force out of you.

The "narcissist", as you can already tell, is a very self-obsessed entity. They are not to be confused with someone who is self-aware. They have the mentality that everything revolves around their existence, and they also have a disregard for others' energy. One very prominent thing about these entities is that they never seem to take others into account. Your wellness means nothing to them; they only regard their own health or lack thereof. Most energy vampires share similar traits and perform in similar ways, but they all have distinctions that we manage to point out.

The "manipulator" is very similar to the rest, but it is an expert in its craft. They will constantly go out of their way to feed you good energy, or that is what we think they are doing. However, this seemingly good energy is rarely well-intentioned. They feed your energy just in order to take from it once again like a farmer overfeeding their livestock just to get more meat from them when they are killed. It is important to be very wary of these types; if they sink their teeth into you once, it will likely happen many times before you even notice what is happening.

Have you ever felt like something or someone has power over your body, mind, and spirit? Well, frankly, we have all felt like that at some point. This happens mainly because the "controller" has entered your space and started extracting from your light. They will try to dominate your energy, and once you have succumbed to their ways, you constantly feel the need to react to their requests in a submissive way.

This type of energy can also make you question yourself, which is not a healthy trait to harbor within your aura. Some entities have submissive energy by nature, and that is when we have to be extra cautious. It is always a good thing to remain true to your authentic energy, but if you have submissive energy, please be vigilant, always remembering to focus on owning and protecting that energy.

The most unpredictable energy vampire is most likely the "split" vampire. You can never be at ease with any sort of energy vampire, but this one especially keeps you on your toes. They never react the same way twice, and their energy switches between positive and negative quite rapidly, leaving you uncertain and often vulnerable to their ways. Their push-and-pull mannerisms also create confusion, which can cause an imbalance in your energy.

Energy vampires are all complex. They might generate their negativity towards only you without having the same effect on others, and no one would be able to provide reasoning for that. They are the only people who can provide those answers. The "attention seeker" type of energy vampire only thrives off appraisal - positive appraisal, that is. They drain the energy of others by constantly drawing sympathy, consideration, and approval from you. These types also demand constant energy to be directed towards them and not shared. They are basically those types that want to be in the spotlight constantly, and this could be an extremely draining force when dealt with.

There is a new brand of energy vampires that exist each and every day, so it can be difficult to avoid them all. The ones mentioned above are some of the more common kinds that most of us encounter or have encountered in our lives. Luckily, the next topic will give you some insight into dealing with these energy vampires in ways that still enable you to own your energy and protect your aura to the fullest extent.

DEALING WITH ENERGY VAMPIRES

We are human beings, and one part of being human is the constant need for social interaction. We often fuse with another being's aura, and that is why our energies and vibrations often connect with each other. The spaces we find ourselves in, especially the social ones, become part of our environments. It would be ideal to live in isolation, but we are not wired that way and never will be. Other entities constantly penetrate our space, and this is not necessarily a bad thing. Most of the time, the encounters we share with other entities can be positive or intuitive and actually nourish our bodies, minds, and spiritual presence.

It is unrealistic to assume that every entity that takes on the form of an energy vampire deserves to be extradited from our lives. The key to enlightenment is to spread the love and light we carry within ourselves to others. Energy vampires are weak, and this is why they feed off our energy. There is a way to influence them positively in order to banish their negativity without banishing them.

Shunning others can also be a negative portrayal of our auras. We must always attempt to use positive reinforcement before expulsion. Taking care of one another and creating a unified environment is more effective than simply excluding everything and everyone that is threatening. Your light can also be a guide to wellness for others in a sustainable way.

You will come to realize that the more confident and resourceful you become during this journey, the harder it will be for things like toxic energy and energy vampires to affect or penetrate your aura. We are adaptable creatures, so it is not always necessary to tune into your self-awareness before you enter a different space. When you are confident in the level of ownership you have over your energy, you will become less and less vulnerable to energy vampires and toxic energy. Your resilience will enable you to consume the same space as them without succumbing to their bad vibrations. They will simply bounce off you.

That is when you have the opportunity to embrace that toxic entity or energy vampire and shine your light over them. Hopefully, it will influence their energy to become less negative and create more opportunities for positive energy to spread.

But before all this is even possible, we must first address why it is even remotely possible for these energy vampires to affect you to this extent. It is in no way possible, in certain situations, to know straight away what this entity's intentions are. As we learned in the previous paragraphs, they are often disguised as loving, confident, and often comforting entities. That is how they manage to open us up and grab a hold of our energy. We will be using examples of hypothetical relationships in order to clarify the concept of the energy vampire's ability to enter our environments.

They often lure us in by disguising themselves as something we would want to include in our space. For example, your romantic partner could adjust their personality to make them more attractive. As soon as they have some sort of control over you, they can either change abruptly or as time goes on. They soon become more and more exhausting to be around, eventually exposing their true colors (no pun intended).

Some energy vampires know how to create a need or demand for their presence by pretending, or even becoming, something that we are missing from our lives. Because most of them have become so good at their craft, they also are intelligent and able to identify certain aspects of our auras or lives. For example, an energy vampire will make you feel a certain way when you are around them. They will try their best to assure that you only feel this way when they are present. They then use this tactic to turn you into a needy person, when in all actuality, they are the needy ones because they feed their energy through your demise.

These energy vampires may also use our problems and suffering as their way in. When we are going through hardships in life, we become less able to do certain things or unable to feel particular emotions. Some of us suffer from chemical imbalances which lead to mental illnesses. Sadly, certain energy vampires can spot that easily and use this to their advantage. An example of this is when your romantic partner is aware of your suffering and uses it against you to win an argument.

They will also manipulate a situation or circumstance by creating a false scenario that requires a change in our lives of some sort. They use this as their way in - by creating a false void and selling themselves as the filler. This is almost like when someone tells you to buy something that you really do not need in order to make money off you, only for you to discover that this product is creating more problems than it is solving, or creating problems by trying to fix issues that were not even there in the beginning.

We all find something positive or comforting in someone/something we can relate to. Energy vampires are pretentious and make us believe certain things about themselves that are not true simply to appear more relatable. When we feel like we share some sort of relationship with a being, it gives us hope, comfort, or plain and simple joy, amongst other things. For example, someone will pretend to have the same problem as you just so that you can feel some sort of bond with them.

There are many possible ways in which an energy vampire can use and abuse their power. Whether they are aware of what they are doing or not is only known to them; we have no way of telling what their intentions are, and sometimes it is hard to identify them because we do not want to think badly of someone. The only true way to protect yourself from their allure is to remain grounded in all your encounters.

Be your authentic self, be open, and be loving. Just as much as you need to remain a source of light and love, you must also practice your ability to be a powerful force of positivity. By the end of this book, you will be fully equipped to do so, because this is your guide, and YOU are an extremely able, magnificent, and courageous intellectual.

❧ 4 ❧
ENERGY PATHOGENS

WHAT ARE ENERGY PATHOGENS?

Our auras and energy are in a permanent state of interaction with other energies, whether they are people, objects, or animals. We are more concerned with the energy exchanges between people because of our natural social wants and needs. From time to time, we soak up other people's energies or parts thereof. Now, we have already discussed toxic energy and energy vampires, but the one thing we have not mentioned is energy pathogens. Within the study of biology, pathogens are usually presentable in forms of fungi, bacteria, viruses, and/or parasites. In simpler terms, a pathogen is an organism that is capable of carrying disease. We also refer to pathogens as germs, a word that we see on every label that has anything to do with cleanliness or medicine.

When it comes to the study of the body, mind, and spirit, we also find pathogens. These particular pathogens, however, are linked to our aura and our energy field. Like most biological pathogens, the energy variety of them is also not something you wish to experience. They also have the ability to cause detrimental auric diseases that can leave your energy field in a very traumatic state.

Energy pathogens are beings that infect the aura with a spiritual and/or mental disease. In simpler terms, energy pathogens affect your aura with such incredible force that it weakens it and causes disease. Yes, we can become physically ill if our aura is affected, but energy pathogens are more closely linked to disease of the mind, body, and spirit. Our auras are already filled with these microbes, though they are virtually harmless unless they become activated or enter a part of the aura that they do not normally reside in.

The energy pathogens that already exist in your aura can become problematic when your energy field is struggling, vulnerable, and dull. This can occur through toxic energy, energy vampires, or other surrounding influences. Feel free to scan through the previous chapters if you feel the need to re-familiarize yourself with those three. Energy pathogens can also enter your aura if they are passed on by another entity or being. If another person is carrying a possible auric disease, they can (and most likely will) pass it on to you if your aura is vulnerable or if you are not careful.

These energy pathogens cannot survive on their own; they usually feed off your body, mind, and spirit in order to thrive. It finds its way in through the energy penetrating your aura. When these pathogens enter the aura, they do not leave in a hurry. Somehow, they find a way to settle in our auras without any issues. Just like your physical body, your aura also has to fight against energy pathogens in order to avoid diseases. When we look at auric sickness, it is usually linked to our feelings, vibrations, emotions, and actions. Yes, they also have an indirect effect on your physical body's wellness.

So as these pathogens remain in your aura, they feed off of it. All the spiritual nourishment you attempt to submit into your aura is eaten away by these hungry leeches, leaving little to no replenishment for your aura. Your energy immediately takes a turn for the worst, and this can leave you vulnerable to a list of other hazardous invaders.

Energy pathogens can be spread through various methods, causing chaos and harm as far as they go. The scary part is, as soon as they are done stripping your aura of all its energy, they leave and find another aura or being to tear apart. It is almost like they are demons that need to find another host once they are done feeding off the soul of the first host. But just like demons, we can get rid of pathogens before it is too late. You do not have to take part in some sort of exorcism, but certain rituals do help. Later on, we will discuss the positive effects rituals have on our auras and how they can aid in the protection and ownership of our energy.

There are various signs that a pathogen has entered your aura and is causing some irreparable damage. You will most likely have to speak or actually pay a visit to a healer in order to pin down the exact cause of your auric illness. If this is not possible for you, then there is no cause for alarm. This chapter will equip you with enough insight to identify and locate a pathogen in your aura.

Later in the book, we will also look at some healing rituals and practices that will help you get rid of the pathogen(s) and restore all the nourishment it stole from your aura. It is important to consider all forms of healing, because this can help you find practices or rituals that can become a constant in your life.

There are some key symptoms that are almost immediate indicators of energy pathogens that have been activated or have infiltrated your aura. When we experience some form of mental or spiritual fatigue, our auras become dull, and the driving force we have within us becomes weak. Toxic energy, energy vampires, and other surrounding influences could be the cause, or some sort of energy pathogen may have entered your aura.

When we encounter an incompatible energy or incompatible energy pathogen, it can cause a state of distress within our inner being. During our stay on Earth, we inhabit these physical bodies, and our auras can be affected by anything they consume. Your physical health, as we already know, can have a very direct effect on your aura, causing an imbalance and various forms of clutter that will overwhelm your current wellness or vitality.

Once your aura becomes infected, the pathogens have the ability to latch on to and attack the parts of your aura that keep it vibrant and forceful. They then use those modules to multiply, which can cause an overcrowding of energy pathogens. As soon as this energy pathogen lets go of the first component, it moves on to the rest, until it has reached every aspect of your aura.

Let us use our mental well-being as an example. If your aura is invaded by an energy pathogen, the first thing you will notice is your positive mental state change to negative. You will start to feel negative emotions towards other entities, leading to negative thoughts, and then negative reactions.

Once you are infected with all this negativity, you will start to unravel. After this energy pathogen has infected all aspects of your wellness, you will feel an overwhelming sense of emotional or mental fatigue, leaving you weak. Your energy will then start to send out negative vibrations.

Just when you think you have had enough and this energy pathogen has become dormant, it strikes again, leaving you feeling hopeless and unable to find the strength to pulsate positive energy. Energy pathogens are extremely diverse. One of these pathogens can be anything that leaves you feeling spiritually imbalanced, mentally unwell, and physically ill. Energy pathogens can also adjust to any environment; just because you are doing well in your life does not mean they cannot invade your aura and rally up some chaos.

These invaders can come from within. When you are reflecting inwards and constantly associate yourself with negativity, you are feeding a part of yourself to an energy pathogen, enabling it to thrive and multiply. This is why it is so crucial to maintain a healthy perspective on your own authentic self. Every now and then, these negative thoughts and ideas we have of ourselves spiral out of control. When you feed the energy pathogen parts of yourself, you are enabling them to infect the neutral energy within your aura.

When dealing with certain energy pathogens, we have to remember that they can become immune to certain forms of healing. That is why it is important to find various attempts to heal your aura and switch it up from time to time. Even small changes to a ritual or habit can be the cure. Energy is constantly in motion, changing all the time. Your aura is also everchanging, and so are you. That is why healing rituals or habits, or methods thereof, can become overused, making it predictable for potential invaders.

Energy pathogens can also be quite docile if they are controlled. As soon as there is too much negativity floating around in our auras, that is when we encounter that sense of crippling anxiety and like we are trapped. This is because this energy pathogen, whether it is bad energy or a physical illness, has become overbearing or consumes too much of our positive vibrations. If you let it grow, it will not go, to put it simply.

Some energy pathogens come as one tiny problem that grows into a massive issue, while some come as one and somehow multiply into various types. Energy pathogens can also contaminate one layer of the aura and move on to different layers or multiply itself until it is present all around.

Your level of control over energy pathogens, as well as your immunity towards them, will rise as you let yourself grow spiritually and mentally. We are not born immune to energy pathogens, and we will most likely never become fully immune to energy pathogens, but we can learn how to interact with them as little as possible.

There is a common misconception that once you have healed completely, you will not be able to be infected by energy pathogens. Our lives, circumstances, and minds are in a constant state of change, and it is never safe to think that we are untouchable. Becoming overly confident in your body, mind, and spirit can be just as detrimental as being too meek or out of control. Once you humble yourself with this idea, you will come to realize that a part of being balanced is also allowing yourself to be fearful in an attempt to protect your energy, but never fearful in an attempt to attack yourself or others.

THE DIFFERENT LAYERS AND COLORS FOUND IN YOUR AURA

In order to know what an unhealthy aura encompasses, we must first be able to identify a healthy aura. When we look at a visual reading of an aura, we can see a whole array of different colors. Each color represents a different trait, quality, or emotion. Your aura can reveal each and every single thing about your existence, whether it is past experiences or your current state of vitality. Your aura also has different layers.

These layers surround your physical body, and when something like an energy pathogen penetrates them, they have the potential to reach your physical body. These energy pathogens are intruders, which you now know can cause physical and mental distress. If your auric field is erratic, it can also be affected by other auras. This means that energy pathogens that have infected another individual's aura can be contagious, in a sense. That is why it is so important to protect your energy and take ownership of your individual aura (Schweitzer, 2013).

In order to understand how pathogens potentially enter the body, we must comprehend both the meaning of different aura colors and the different bodies or layers. When we can grasp the anatomy of the aura, it will become easier to identify potential threats within your own aura and the energy fields of other beings. You might not be able to see the aura of others, but detecting the vibrations that they are giving off will give you a sense of their current auric state.

The first layer we will discuss is the etheric layer. This layer is the one that sits the closest to our physical body. Our organs and tissues are attached to this layer. The cells that are constantly dying or growing in our physical bodies are closely aligned with the etheric layer. This is why we can become physically ill if an energy pathogen is able to reach this level of the aura.

Second is the emotional layer. It is the second auric level and is located just outside of the etheric body. It contains all of our emotions, like anger, joy, sorrow, love, and many others. As we already know, this layer can become quite cluttered because of our human ability to experience various emotions all at once. This also explains why this layer is in constant motion and color variation. The danger of an energy pathogen penetrating it can be quite devastating for your emotional well-being.

The mental layer is located directly outside the emotional body or layer. It holds all of our mental capacity. The thoughts that we experience and process are found in the mental layer, such as judgment, admiration, restraint, and ideas. Energy pathogens that enter this layer usually affect our mental health systems.

The fourth layer is known as the astral layer. It acts as a bridge between our lower vibrational field (physical) and our elevated vibrational field (spiritual). Most of the energy we exchange with others through interaction comes from this layer and also reaches it. Energy pathogens that invade this layer can have an effect on our relationships or interactions with others.

The etheric template represents a map of the body, almost like a blueprint. It creates an empty, or negative, space for the etheric layer to form. Some healers are able to detect problems with the physical body by analyzing the etheric template. This is also where an energy pathogen is likely to either remain or move on to the next layer.

The second-to-last layer is the celestial body which connects us to the universe. In chakra terms, it is connected to the third eye. This is also where your spiritual connection is anchored and your whole existence is entering the development of enlightenment. Energy pathogens that infiltrate it can cause a spiritual imbalance.

The final layer, number seven, is known as the spiritual layer. It is the protector of the remaining layers and is, therefore, your shield. When you have a healthy and balanced aura, it will strengthen this and make it nearly impossible for energy pathogens to get far enough to affect your other layers.

An aura contains a different array of colors, and they can be representative of your true self, true feelings, spiritual wellness, and many other identifiers.

When the color red is present in your aura, it is usually associated with strong energy, well-grounded thoughts, an active presence, and many other strong attributes.

Orange is usually a signifier of bravery, a considerate personality, self-assurance, and an adventurous spirit.

Yellow, depending on its brightness, can mean that there is joy, playfulness, sensitivity, and some fragility involved.

Green is most likely associated with nature and peace; it is a sign of a nurturing spirit and someone with a need for social interaction.

Blue is seen as helpful, spiritual, and in tune with the universe and themselves. Blue is also associated with beings that are understanding and can be overwhelmed because of their empathetic nature.

Indigo auras are representative of a dreamer, gentleness, and modesty. Violet, which can be close to Indigo on the color palette, is known as a wise and very sensitive being. Some also believe that beings with violet auras have psychic abilities.

Please note that these are general ideas, and colors can carry a bunch of different meanings. For an accurate reading of your aura, it is advised that you visit a healer or a reader who is trained to do so. There are also a variety of teachings that you can pursue in order to enable yourself to do it. Your aura's color is usually a depiction of your body, soul, mind, and spirit. As we interact with different color auras, we draw various types of energy from them. To some, a red aura can be intimidating, but to others, it could be inspiring.

When we look at an unhealthy aura, it can be a signifier that the entity who the aura surrounds is in some sort of distress. Auras that have been infected by an energy pathogen are easy to distinguish. They will usually lose the vibrancy of their aura. This can cause dull, gray, or dark color variations. The shape of their aura, which should ideally be shaped like an egg, will appear patchy or jagged. It can also have protrusions and dents in it.

When you start recognizing these signifiers in your own or others' auras, proceed with caution and pay attention to it as soon as possible. Energy does not lie, and neither does one's aura.

❈ 5 ❈

NEUTRALIZING YOUR ENERGY

REDUCING NEGATIVE ENERGY

Having negative energy affecting your aura and also invading your physical space (like your home and your body) can trigger certain health problems. In the previous chapter, we discussed how the aura is made up of seven levels. These levels (etheric, emotional, mental, astral, etheric template, celestial body, and etheric body) surround you like a halo of sorts. In order to maintain a well-balanced aura, it is crucial to consider using certain rituals or therapies as they can aid you in the cleansing process.

These practices are usually performed by enlightened healers, and, as we already know, a vibrant aura can result in a vibrant life. Your overall well-being and the way you emit and receive different energy from your inner self and even from others can surely benefit from these practices. There are many of these, as well as therapies, which are available to us. They are also easily accessible and supposedly not as financially draining as modern medicine.

Let us start by looking at the holistic approach to overall health. This approach, unlike some other forms of healing, focuses on the human as a whole. It does not only account for the physical body, but considers the body, mind, and spirit.

For example, if you find yourself experiencing a period of uncertainty, you can seek out holistic methods to figure out how to solve this uncertainty by assessing all aspects instead of just focusing on one problem or concern. If your mental state feels at all off, it affects your physical and mental state.

When taking a look at holistic medicine, you will notice that it addresses the well-being of the person in totality. It analyzes your physical, mental, and emotional/spiritual health while also assessing surrounding influences. When you are seeking a verdict or diagnosis, all possible symptoms are taken into account for a medical explanation or reasoning.

Holistic treatment or therapies enable us to gain more control over the healing process by empowering and encouraging us to use our aura and energy to our advantage. It might be an alternative route to modern medicine, but it has proven to be just as sufficient and arguably more sustainable than we might realize.

The holistic approach starts at the very core of the issue at hand. The first step is to outline the problem and then reflect on it as a whole. Like most things in life, the reasoning behind certain difficulties can be unpredictable. We might think we have the answers to everything, but as we have discovered in previous chapters, we do not. A holistic approach enables us to identify all signifiers or causes, which can lead to a more stable solution or treatment.

In order to solve certain dilemmas and hardships, it is important to keep an open mind. Functional fluidity excludes the idea that what may have helped before might work again. Sometimes it is needed to compromise in order to come to an agreed-upon solution. Opening ourselves up and loosening our grip can enable us to think outside of the norm and discover other remedies that might provide us with better results. For this to work, one must remain open to all possibilities, even if we are not instantly convinced.

What we think is happening versus what is actually happening is a tale as old as time. Our reality, or what we perceive as reality, might not always be accurate because our thoughts or feelings towards something could be influenced by something else. If we attempt to identify a problem during a time of distress, it could cloud our judgment, and the problem we have identified might be inaccurate.

This is why it is essential to neutralize our emotions during a crisis and evaluate the possible problem by disregarding our influenced or clouded perceptions of what it might be. Being level-headed during these periods can make it easier to find a solution because the information we absorb is most likely accurate or relevant to the situation.

Assumptions can be very detrimental when we are dealing with different issues or conflicts. Similar to clouded judgment, assumptions are not always concrete evidence of what is occurring. If we disregard the assumptions that we made based on our thoughts or understandings, it can open up a door for more truthful information to pass through. This can be helpful during times when we feel conflicted.

It is human nature to divert the blame away from ourselves, and sometimes we are not to blame. However, as we discussed before, some situations occur when we do not take responsibility for our energy. When we are addressing a problem, especially when it involves another person, we tend to react in our own defense instead of addressing the issue at hand from a neutral perspective. In order to neutralize the situation, we must drop our defensive attitude toward the issue or person and react in an impartial manner. Being in control of our emotions when we encounter negativity can enable us to come up with solutions that benefit us in the long run.

It is easy to ignore certain issues or aspects that might make us uncomfortable, but when we push these thoughts or this negativity further and further down, it will eventually bounce back with more impact. We have to listen to our problems in an active sense. When we are actively addressing negative energy, it can release this trapped energy and relieve our auras of emotional or mental clutter.

Constantly neglecting our inner thoughts or conflicts will only result in a flash flood of negativity that will eradicate all possible solutions. The only way to find a solution is to identify the true cause of a certain situation or issue. It usually helps to think of the problem and then say it out loud to yourself. Once it has exited your consciousness it will relieve you of that negative energy. It is also important not to criticize yourself but rather confront yourself or another being empathetically.

Reiki healing is another form of energy work that can balance, neutralize, and heal your aura. It is a very popular healing method and is known for its definite results. Reiki comes from Rei (God's wisdom) and Ki (energy) and stems from Japanese. It is a very effective method to use alongside or together with traditional medicines or healing methods and therapies. During reiki sessions, energy is used to heal the person's body, mind, and spirit. A lot of holistic practices are similar in this way because they focus on all aspects of the aura instead of taking a one-sided approach.

These therapies require mostly a flow of energy through the hands of the healer and specific hand movement techniques. Symbolism is used to manifest the energy that we need from the universe, in order to heal or balance out negative energy. The technique used with the hands is usually referred to as palm-healing or hands-on treatment.

Reiki is known to work on every layer of the aura and can be a very enlightening experience for some. It has become more and more popular over the years because there is no evidence that states that it is an unsuccessful treatment method. Those who have experienced reiki therapy or do it ritualistically will most likely suggest trying it before any other healing/cleansing therapies.

Reiki even has the ability to cure physical illnesses because of its use of energy to heal the aura. Cold, flu, and stomach problems, as well as more serious illnesses, have been improved with the help of reiki healing. Although, when it comes to fatal or serious diseases, it is always suggested to try reiki along with modern medicine or as an alternative.

When the universal energy is transferred through the hands of the healer, it enters the various layers of the aura, exploring the possible negativity. Then, once this energy identifies the problem, it neutralizes it. Seeing that reiki is a form of energy healing, it has the ability to fill your aura with relaxing, emotionally content and overall positive energy, which then creates a healing process within your different aura layers. This balances the aura and restores its vibrancy and luminosity, which are the signifiers of a healthy and enriched aura.

It is believed to be a very relaxing therapy, and some people make use of it just to relax and de-stress. Aside from all the mentioned benefits, it also helps to treat various types of mental illnesses, heart disease, cancer, chronic pain, and infertility. It is also believed that reiki therapy can help those with autism and Crohn's disease, only further proving that reiki is a very effective form of energy healing (Newman, 2017).

Qigong therapy is a form of therapy that is also considered very effective in restoring balance to the aura. It has been used for around 4,000 years and originated in China as a form of traditional healing and medicine. Qigong involves certain movements that accompany each other and also includes breathing practices and various forms of meditation to increase auric health and overall physical health. It is also known to soothe and stimulate the spiritual body of the aura and use positive energy to achieve its wondrous outcomes.

Traditional Chinese healers and the study of traditional Chinese medicine assert that wellness is achieved if the "yin" and "yang" of our energy force is balanced. This energy force is known as our "qi" (pronounced "chi"), and it is believed that most ailments exist when these forces are not well-balanced (Brazier, 2017).

Our qi moves through meridians, or gateways, throughout our physical bodies, and so does our energy. They can be reached through 350 acupuncture points in the physical body. Acupuncture therapy is extremely popular and practiced very often for many different reasons. Acupuncture needles are gently placed into these points with meticulous intent and are said to balance out the energy flow.

Numerous studies and witnesses have shown that acupuncture therapy is an effective treatment for many different conditions. Neuroscience has explained acupuncture as a therapy that uses certain points for healing, because it is located near nerves, muscles, and connective tissue. It helps to increase energy and blood flow throughout the physical body and is believed to awaken the body and enable it to combat pain points naturally.

Having needles put inside your body for a certain amount of time sounds quite scary, but it is actually not painful and does not cause as much distress as one might imagine. Because these needles are placed strategically and not too deep, it can be a very relaxing and rejuvenating experience. The healer or acupuncturist will start by examining and assessing the patient and practice active listening in order to calculate what form of acupuncture will be best suited for their condition. After that, a very sterile arrangement of thin needles is placed in certain acupuncture points.

When you undergo this form of therapy, you will most likely lie down to assure that energy flows through your body evenly and that the therapist has access to the points in need of attention. It might be a tingly or dull and temporarily uncomfortable, but it is regarded as a fairly painless procedure. The session can last between five and thirty minutes depending on your condition. The amount of times you have to go through the procedure also is determined by your condition. Some people prefer to do it ritualistically for aura maintenance.

Acupuncture is considered a safe treatment with very few side effects, if any at all. It can also be added to other treatments for efficiency and is safe to combine with various forms of healing. It is known to be a natural way to control or even stop certain types of inflammation in the physical body that causes pain and discomfort. If you are unable or unwilling to try modern medicine, this approach to healing is an ideal way to banish the negativity that is often stored in the aura and physical body (Brazier, 2017).

Some other healing methods to consider are pranic healing and crystal healing. Pranic healing focuses exclusively on using the body's life force to heal the aura and energy field. It focuses exclusively on the energy and aura, prioritizing the different levels of the aura as its reference. It then uses positive energy reinforcement to remove toxins from the aura, which ultimately leads to physical healing as well.

Crystal healing is a very aesthetically pleasing healing method. Various precious stones and crystals are used to pull the negativity from the body when placed upon certain points, and then they proceed to banish this negativity and extract certain filths. Various stones and crystals carry different healing properties, and they are usually extremely easy to come by.

❧ 6 ❧
BIOFIELDS AND DIFFERENT
THERAPIES

E very living being, especially the ones on planet Earth, is made and designed with the capability of healing itself. It is rumored that healers and civilians have used energy fields for thousands of years in order to establish certain diagnoses.

Auric, or biofield healing, therapies were developed early on and used as identifiers and healing methods for pain, cellular rejuvenation, immune boosting, and, of course, spiritual healing.

Lately, biofield therapies have started becoming more and more exposed thanks to certain scientific studies. It has also been intertwined with western or modern medicine treatments in order to aid the healing process.

The biofield is a very large stream of energy that exudes out from our physical bodies and can extend up to eight feet. It cannot necessarily be seen, but it has been recorded that it is possible to feel it whenever there is a change in temperature or some sort of pressure release or input is involved. We already know that some healers (even those who do not practice healing) are capable of seeing our auras change color, but not all therapies involved with our biofields involve the reading of these various colors or levels.

Biofield healing, or as others may call it, "information medicine", is becoming a more common treatment/therapy among modern people. This is due to the decline in western medicine's credibility and many pharmaceutical companies that have been exposed for selling unnecessary chemical compounds.

People have also turned to energy healing therapies because of how inexpensive they are and their overall success rates. It has been proven countless times by witnesses and by patients themselves that holistic medicine, especially medicine that focuses on energy, is an effective way to treat certain issues, whether they are physical, mental, or spiritual.

The biofield, just like the aura, is the energy that surrounds the body. It can act as a shield against various other energies and vibrations. The biofield surrounding us is also capable of identifying every aspect of our existence, whether it is a memory, emotion, or illness. The existence of a biofield even goes as far back as 1939, when Harold Saxon Burr, Ph.D., and F.S.C. Northrup suggested that every physical entity has an electrodynamic field surrounding it that suggests life (2018).

We know by now that there are various devices that can depict the energy fields that radiate from our bodies. It usually works with electromagnetic systems. Some believe that this sort of research does not receive proper funding due to its holistic nature, but lately, the support towards energy healing has been increasing and its popularity rising. Due to various surrounding influences like pollution, politics, and other outward problems, people have been exploring more natural approaches to healing.

Understandably so, this modern life has released an extreme amount of toxins into the world, and it is natural for us and our energies to seek out healthier approaches. Whenever you think you are experiencing a "gut-feeling", it is just your biofield or aura communicating with you. That is why it is so important to be open towards this communication and always participate (2018).

It is common during biofield therapy to only attempt to deal with the highest good of the patient or client. Any therapy regarding the biofield is non-invasive; it only takes care of the energy surrounding the body. This basically means that even though a surgeon can recommend biofield or energy healing, it is not and will never be a surgical procedure. These healing methods or therapies are mostly done by healers who specialize in the various forms.

Biofield therapy usually requires the patient to lay down so that the field can be easily assessed, and the therapist or healer will tap into the patient's energy or biofield by using only their hands. There are even some healers who do not touch the patients and can read or diagnose the patient merely through this approach.

These therapies are mostly used to reduce stress and anxiety because it is believed to be linked closely to their physical health, as well. This is true in most cases because, as we learned before, our energy can and possibly always does, have a direct effect on our physical bodies. Many also seek the services of healers or therapists in order to prevent certain issues before they even exist.

These prevention methods can often be successful if the client or patient has a certain history with these problems. However, overall prevention therapy is also a popular approach to energy or biofield therapy. Many patients and clients use these biofield therapies after they have struggled with some sort of ailment or illness as a way to add to the medicine they already use. As we learned in previous chapters, this is extremely common these days and is often said to be a very effective way to deal with certain health issues.

Many view these therapies as an overall way of improving your health - almost like taking vitamins and supplements on the daily, it is also extremely common for people to remedy physical injuries or other physical issues with biofield therapy. Biofield therapies, depending on the legitimacy of your healer or general practitioner, can be used for pretty much anything, whether it is maintaining your health or improving it, reducing stress, or channeling a different part of yourself - basically anything goes.

These therapies, like other holistic therapies, are effective and attainable without being overly expensive and direct. There are certain therapies that focus on specific issues, but most biofield therapies are extremely versatile and flexible. Although it might seem too good to be true, it has been proven to be an effective form of adjunctive healing and has even been proven to work as an individual approach on its own.

Three of the most common biofield therapies are reiki healing, healing touch, and therapeutic touch. In the previous chapter, we discussed reiki healing fairly briefly. It is, however, one of the most popular biofield therapies. Pranic healing is also a method that some use, but it has been proven to be quite scarce and not as popular as reiki or certain touch therapies.

As previously mentioned, they are quite effective without being invasive, and one never feels pain or discomfort during or after the procedure. In support of conventional or alternative medicine, some of these therapies are starting to become useful in even more serious healing spaces, like hospitals, which were said to have been reluctant for very long. However, there should be more research done to establish the details of why and how it works, exactly.

In the previous chapter, we also glanced at reiki healing as a form of reducing negative energy. Reiki is also a very popular biofield therapy. It has become extremely well-known among western society over the years, most likely due to its lack of invasiveness and highly effective nature. It originated in Japan during the early 1900s and requires the practitioner or healer to open up their patient to the healing energy that comes from the universe.

The universal life force is actually the true healer, not the master or practitioner themselves. You do not necessarily need to believe in it for it to work. This universal life force can penetrate any biofield, and disbelief is not considered an energy block when it comes to reiki. Reiki masters use about twelve or thirteen hand gestures, mostly linked to chakras, in order to complete the therapy.

It does not stem from any specific religion, but it does remain a mixture of spiritual and healing therapy. Because of its religious neutrality, it has no specific outcome to keep in mind. One should only focus on the healing process and not the approach itself. It is believed to be a very enriching experience, and many think it has the ability to restore balance in the biofield or aura.

Reiki masters usually undergo three levels of training before becoming masters of practicing healers. It often occurs through lineages, but it also has a professional association that oversees proper education and ethics. It is called The Association of Reiki Professionals. This organization ensures that it is properly performed and that there are no involvements that can affect the practitioner or client/patient negatively in any way. This organization also ensures that these healers receive the proper training and education that is required to become a healer (and is in such high demand lately).

Healing touch is another widely performed biofield therapy offered globally. It supposedly originated in 1989 and was founded by Janet

Mentgen who was also a certified nurse. It is known to be a more linear or rigid therapy than reiki due to its structural nature (2018). During this approach, the healing is done by both the practitioner and the client, unlike reiki where the healing is done by the universal life force and the two physical beings are just there to send and receive that force or energy.

It is also considered to be a less spiritual process, although many feel that the spirituality aspect remains prevalent throughout. The healing takes place because it creates a switch in energy that is enabled by touch. It is said to be a supervised method that has to follow strict instructive information to work.

Different positions are used in a hands-on approach, these hand positions depend on what the client or patient is asking for even depending on the diagnosis. Different hand positions work in different ways to transport energy onto different parts. These practitioners follow these supervised methods of this approach in order for the healing process to be successful. Healing therapy is divided into five essential modules that a prospective healer must complete in order to become a certified healer or practitioner. Healing touch therapy is said to help those with certain mental, physical, and spiritual disorders. It is also famous for the effects it has on those suffering from anxiety disorders, depression, issues reduced from trauma, chronic or allocated pain, and certain cancer symptoms.

Pranic healing is arguably the most spiritually-inclined healing method when it comes to biofield therapies. It was established by Grandmaster Chao Kok Sui, and it usually embodies both the biofield and the use of chakras. It also makes use of color variations and crystals to encourage healing and identifying issues involved with the biofield. It is believed to be more intricate than most biofield therapies and requires more extensive training and practices.

There are a minimum of five to six training levels and also the use of manuals in conjunction with specific steps that have to be considered when this therapy is approached. Because of its detoxifying nature, it is a closely maintained and supervised training process so as to prevent a possible slip-up that could drain the biofield of its energy, for example. It follows a linear approach that is extremely organized, delicate, and meticulous. It is rumored that there are only a few practitioners left that practice this sort of healing.

Therapeutic touch (not to be confused with reiki healing or healing touch) is another form of biofield healing therapy. It existed before healing touch and originated in the 1970s. It was founded by nursing professor Dolores Krieger and a healer named Dora Kunz in New York City (2018). It is believed to be the first concept that directly linked healing and healthcare.

There are not a whole lot of therapeutic touch practitioners left who focus on this approach or method alone; most healers add certain aspects to other biofield therapies seeing that this is one of the foundations for energy healing methods. A lot of practitioners combine therapeutic touch techniques with healing touch energy, which is more likely to appear in biofield healing practices today (2018).

Recently, we have seen a lot more biofield therapies popping up globally, some with all new ways to approach your biofield and identify certain issues. Bio-tuning, for example, is a fairly new treatment that makes use of sound to heal the biofield. During a biofield tuning session, the client lies down while the specialized practitioner puts the handles of vibrating tuning forks on specific points on the client's body. The practitioner or healer also slowly moves these hovering tuning forks over the patient's body. The vibrations that the body sends off will then cause these forks to make certain sounds that can indicate whether the client is welcoming certain vibrations or resisting them.

The resistance or force that was apprehended in that specific area is then disbanded and reintroduced into circulation. It is believed to re-tune the vibrations inside our bodies to become balanced and restored. The practice of treating these areas of resistance in a patient's energy field creates aimed and immediate stimulation that apparently helps the patient with certain issues.

Whatever biofield healing practice we use to heal, prevent, or balance out certain problems can be based on our location and our views. We do know that certain practices can work for almost anything, while others have the ability to hone in on specific issues and approach them singularly.

﹩ 7 ﹩

MODERN SOCIAL SLAVERY

MEDIA CONTROL AND COLLECTIVE CONSCIOUSNESS

The term media describes the communication outlets we use to spread, store, and organize certain information or data. There are various kinds of media. For example, magazines and newspapers fall under print media, and the news some of us watch in the evenings is considered to be broadcasting media. Anything that provides information or data to the public with a specific purpose can be referred to as media.

Mass media communication has been around for centuries, and we rely on it to provide us with information regarding the world we live in on a daily basis. It is a powerful tool that can often be used to disadvantage some, while others gain from it. It is also a very fruitful industry for investors due to advertisements and endorsements that manipulate the system to advantage them and/or their cause.

In the previous chapters, we learned that surrounding influences have the ability to affect our energy a great deal. One of these surrounding influences that has proven itself extremely impactful is the media. These surrounding influences are the main generators of our lives. One could even argue that they help generate the energy we produce. Our surrounding influences shape most of our attitudes or beliefs towards certain things, and with the media being one of them, it often uses information to influence these attitudes and beliefs.

There is a certain way that these influences can mold our wants and needs. The information we surround ourselves with has the ability to fabricate our reality. For example, if we constantly surround ourselves with information regarding celebrities, it is most likely because we are watching or reading what they do. Your energy feeds off the things you surround yourself with, whether it is good or bad information. The amount or level of contact we allow ourselves to have with these outside influences like the media will ultimately control how often or how much it affects our energy. We do, however, live in a modern society where the media is handled in a more forceful nature because it is literally everywhere we look and everywhere we go.

As we grow up and grow old, the information we have obtained, presently obtain, and possibly will obtain is going to mold our realities. We then carry on shaping our beliefs, opinions, attitudes, and other daily thought processes around this information. Consumerism and certain aspects of politics use the media, for example, to get people to vote for them or purchase their products. The more we swallow the information that media outlets provide us with, the more we curate our realities around them.

Social media, for example, has seen exponential growth over the past few years. We treat it as a news source, a form of social exchange, a visual stimulant, and many other things. Little do we know that it actually influences our thought process so much so that we are rarely in control of it anymore. Our minds are like sponges that are sucking up this information in order for it to keep us hooked on this false reality.

It is such a cliché to assume that the media has the ability to affect our energy, but independent thought is extremely important when it comes to owning your energy and protecting your aura.

The media has enslaved our minds to such an extent that it is impossible for us to stray or refrain from using technology in any way or form. We often do not even think of how much time we spend on our computers, phones, or any other devices on a daily basis. There is nothing wrong with checking up on social media or chatting with a loved one, but we seem to have lost the will to connect with each other in other ways. It is impossible to survive in this modern world without some sort of technological machinery to guide us.

Businesses, essential services, artists, and many other professions are also dependent on social media services to maintain their careers in this consumerist world. However, when trying to identify the reasoning behind this, it always seems to expose itself as enslavement techniques that big industries use to keep us "hooked" on their products. Our fast-paced lives are also to blame, as we simply no longer have the time to balance interaction and relaxation separately. These toxic channels of information have become the fastest accessible way to experience true leisure, because many argue that the only way they can relax is by consuming some sort of product that a medium has put out for them to "enjoy".

Because certain forms of media profit from our participation or consumerism, they have to find ways to keep us entertained and constant throughout the process. These days, technology has become more and more customizable in order to keep an individual hooked on its services or whatever information it sends out. This makes us believe that we are consuming so much relevant information when in actuality, we are just buying into the information that they provide.

Social media, especially, keeps us hooked on its unpredictability. Social media platforms are overpacked with individuals who share, post, and comment continuously. Thanks to our curious human natures, we are hooked on always being aware of what others are doing, making their efforts to keep us from staying away for too long quite successful. Social media, in particular, floods us with information constantly. It is a consistent provider and can often feed us full of incorrect information.

Throughout this book, we constantly repeat the dangers of assumptions, and it is unbelievable how our ability to assume anything about everything is highly enabled and, in fact, encouraged through the media. For example, if we see someone living a very wealthy and spiritual life, traveling the world, and also maintaining an attractive appearance, we automatically perceive that to be their life, without any sense of false assumptions being made.

This becomes highly dangerous because, if your mind is in a certain struggle, it could affect the way you view your own life. You might assume that since you lack all those things the people presented in the media do not, then you are inadequate or not living your life well enough.

The media also has some impact on our consciousness, especially the collective consciousness. Collective consciousness is the central sociological concept that is linked to our shared beliefs, ideas, attitudes, and knowledge that are common in social groups or society. The collective consciousness feeds our sense of belonging and has some sort of link to our identity and often the way we behave in certain instances. It was first described by Emile Durkheim in order to emphasize how we may all be unique, but we are still grouped together into collective spaces, explaining aspects like societies, social groups, and other forms of social or special interaction (Cole, 2019).

As Durkheim further explained throughout his studies, we form societies and certain collective groups because it can make us feel safer and more able to experience solidarity in a sense. It acts as a sort of safety net against the outside dangers of the world. Without communities and functional societies, we would not be able to form this collective consciousness that also acts as a source of solidarity and unity, things that we as highly social creatures are extremely dependent on (Cole, 2019).

The concept of a collective consciousness was first introduced in Durkheim's book *The Division of Labor in Society*, where he stated that collective consciousness is the totality of beliefs and sentiments common to the average members of society. He also studied various traditional and primitive societies, religions, discourses, beliefs, and rituals and found that they harbored the collective consciousness. This caused some sort of homogeneity amongst them and mechanical solidarity. In other words, they automatically bonded together because they shared the same beliefs and other societal concepts. It is still extremely common for us to form mechanical solidarity today, as we have witnessed in various societies globally.

On the other hand, he also observed organic solidarity which proved that societies can also form based on a mutual reliance that they may have on others in order for their society to function properly, which makes the concept of politics come to mind. The religions these societies followed were still the main drivers behind collective consciousness, but other aspects also played an important role to establish this solidarity which was more complex because it was not necessarily a mechanical process (Cole, 2019). Various other institutions, not just religious ones, were also responsible for forming a sense of collective consciousness within a certain soci- ety. These institutions include the state which creates political campaigning and thinking as well as popular media, which we know is a very strong force behind collective consciousness because it tells us how to dress, what to like, and what to eat, and it can influence us in many other ways.

Institutions like the police and educational institutions are also drivers behind collective consciousness but are usually not necessarily ill-inten- tioned or trying to force us to consume certain products or live a certain life. Collective consciousness even has rituals that prove its existence like weddings, sporting events, festivals, and even dining in restaurants (Cole, 2019).

Whether collective consciousness appears in primitive or modern soci- eties, it is always there. It is mostly caused by surrounding influences, and the more we submit to these influences as we grow, older the less we notice that it is a conscious thing. Children are not born with the same collective consciousness; it is something that is taught or forced upon us, a lot of times without us even noticing it. We internalize outside influences or surrounding influences, and that is why it becomes a reality to us.

For example, many western households had a set of rules that have been enforced upon us since we were young. Whether it was school, religion, or just everyday chores, we were taught that it is what we must do and priori- tize in order to live our lives in a well-mannered way. That is also why it is so easy for us to become influenced by popular media; our minds are not used to thinking individualistically unless it is taught to do so.

When it comes to protecting and owning your energy, it is important to be able to think outside of collective consciousness and more individualisti- cally. Individualistic thought will open up certain channels for your own unique energy to flow through. When we focus too much of our energy on collective consciousness, it can enable outside or surrounding influences to affect our body, mind, and spirit even more than it already does.

There can be so many forms of energy pathogens, vampires, and toxic energy floating around in the media we consume in our daily lives. This is not only considering social media, but all forms of media. It clutters our aura with energy-junk that does not necessarily have to be there. What we often tend to ignore, whether consciously or subconsciously, is that we can control the amount of media we allow into our auric space or how much energy we invest or submit towards it.

A regulated or healthy amount of media attention or participation per day is healthy. Although, the moment we over-invest or let it affect our energy too heavily is when we open ourselves up to potential modern social slavery. We can become easily addicted and affected by social media and, like many other forms of negative energy, it is capable of affecting the aura negatively.

An example or possible scenario where this occurs is when we are scrolling through social media and we come across something that instigates conflict or any sort of negative energy from someone. Often reading or witnessing the opinions or disagreements of others obviously causes some sort of negative energy force to consume either ourselves or the space we are occupying. Sometimes just by engaging with certain media platforms, we enable negative energy to harvest and it can latch on to anything or anyone if we do not find a way to rid ourselves of the ability to become media slaves. As we discussed in previous chapters, energy can come from anything, and various mediums are no exception.

When the negativity harvested by exposing ourselves to certain media topics affects our energy, it can and probably will affect our behavior, too. Most media experts know how to use their platforms in order to evoke certain feelings that we carry inside our emotional layers. When these are highly active, like when something makes us extremely emotional, it can cause us to behave in a way that exposes these feelings.

We might read about a certain topic in the newspaper which causes us to feel angry or sad and later react with distress towards someone or indulge in a bucket of ice cream because it extracted a certain feeling out of us, causing a reaction. Some cases can be more serious than others, and certain feelings or experiences tend to spiral out of control. Therefore, it is important not to let too much negative energy affect you through the media you choose to consume.

LOOSENING THE GRIPS OF THE MEDIA

There are many ways to protect your energy from the media. We do not always realize how in control we are of our energy and our aura until we put this control into good use. When we consciously choose which media we will be consuming, it can help us loosen the tight grip that the media and its different forms have on us. If a certain platform often leaves you feeling anxious, regretful, negative, emotionally fatigued, or just overwhelmed, then it is best to avoid it. It manifests negativity, and no matter how hard we try to ignore that negative energy, it will expose itself.

As mentioned above, individual thought is tremendously important in the process of owning and protecting your energy. There are so many media outlets that aim to build and shape your consciousness through opinions and sometimes facts. Yes, it is important to consider factual information, but it is more important to be individualistic and your authentic self. This is the only way you can hold on to the ownership you have over your energy.

When we do consume media, we should try to dwell on the thought it produces instead of reacting or letting it reside instantly. You can process it on your own or by sharing it with others in order to gather more ideas about it. Just be careful because if there is negative energy floating around in that medium, it can affect others negatively, too. The last thing we want to do is spread toxic energy. It can be very effective to process information before letting it manifest. Consciously deciding how it is making you feel or react proves that you have ownership over your energy.

Media rarely holds its fame for sending out positive vibrations, which leaves it up to us. Everyone consumes media, in many forms, and this is why it is important to spread positivity in a world where negativity is the norm. In order to promote positive encounters, you can make an effort to be a positive surrounding influence. Even by just being kind to strangers, you harvest the ability to radiate positive energy into the world, and it also helps you manifest positivity within yourself. Ultimately, this can take away the negative power of the media.

Becoming more proactive in changing the causes and effects of topics in the media or the media itself can also impact the way we consume media, because we become part of the solution. We often shift the blame to others. In this book, the concept of taking responsibility for your energy and behavior is repeated shamelessly. The reason why is that once we take responsibility and become more active in changing our surroundings, it can empower us and others to do the same.

If you have a positive influence or evoke positive energy in someone/something else, it creates a sort of emotional reward system towards yourself. This is simply because doing something good makes you feel good. For example, if there is something in the media that causes negative energy, try to go out and change it. No, it is not always possible to change something that is out of our control, but we are not always fully aware of the impact our energy can have on the world.

❧ 8 ❧
SAFE LIVING AND POSITIVE
VIBRATIONS

Throughout this chapter, we will look at various aspects of our lives that could enhance or improve the energy we send out. There are some things that we tend to neglect or take for granted because they are ritualistic. Sleep, nutrition, exercise, and relationships, among other things, are important factors that feed into and form our energy.

If they are off-balance, then our energy and auras also tend to be imbalanced. You might think to yourself, "duh", but sometimes when something is too obvious, it becomes an afterthought (and when it becomes an afterthought, we do not pay any attention to it). That is how we start to neglect our body, mind, and spirit collectively.

As we now know, our physical body and our surrounding bodies (biofield/aura) are extremely dependent on each other. The impacts they can and do have on one another should not be ignored or taken lightly. In the long run, when we learn to work on the core or "obvious" aspects of our lives, the surrounding things will start to exist in conjunction with the rest. This is why so many healthcare professionals also believe in a balance between physical, mental, and often spiritual rituals in order to maintain a healthy lifestyle.

As humans, we tend to become obsessed with one, but not the other. Yes, they all benefit each other, but if you neglect one part of yourself, then you have to substitute it with the other. Unfortunately, we become more inclined towards the one which we think benefits us the most. Some people become obsessed with fitness and overwork their physical bodies, neglecting their spiritual bodies. On the other side, we often get people who only pay attention to their spiritual bodies and neglect their physical bodies. It can turn into a very vicious and contradicting cycle if we do not pay special attention to it.

To force an ideal upon ourselves that is purely based on unrealistic expectations is extremely ineffective. We are not masters of the universe, and we will never be able to live a 100 percent problem-free life, but we can try our best to come as close to it as possible. A part of being a balanced entity is accepting that everything cannot be great or precise all the time, and it is always our responsibility to check on the energy we send out into the world.

Firstly, we have to take responsibility for the actions we perform on ourselves. If you constantly push yourself over the edge in order to reach a certain goal, then you are opening yourself up to negative energy, or being the negative energy in your own life. Working hard can be extremely rewarding, but it can also be just as draining. We might think that we are moving towards a successful life, but in actuality, we are draining ourselves before we even get there. Becoming a well-balanced entity and maintaining powerful energy is often a challenging journey as we already know. That is why we should remember not to deprive ourselves or overcompensate for anything or anyone.

Sleep is something that most of us take for granted without being fully aware of exactly how beneficial it can be for our physical bodies and our energy. Sleep helps to restore and restock everything that we seem to lose during our daily activities. It gives our bodies time to rebuild our auras and restore the nourishment that we tend to lose when we go through our daily lives. Even if you are not someone who participates in strenuous exercises, your body still needs to rejuvenate itself and build up new energy in preparation for when you awake. When we sleep, our conscious minds have the chance to take a break of some sort. This can be an effective way for our mental layer to recalculate and restore what may have been lost or damaged throughout the day.

Sleep also acts as a rejuvenation and restoration process for the physical body. There has been scientific evidence showing how important sleep is for the body's functionality and protection. It has been proven that certain entities, like animals, can lose all the functions and abilities of their immune systems once they are deprived of sleep. This eventually leads to illness and disease, which can mean a fatal ending for some.

Our physical bodies need sleep to activate certain major physical restorative functions, like muscle growth, tissue restoration, protein fusion, and the release of a majority of growth hormones that mostly or only react during the times our physical bodies are asleep (Why Do We Sleep, Anyway? | Healthy Sleep, 2007).

If our physical bodies do not flourish, our energy can become extremely impacted, leading to an array of other linked side effects. More revitalizing parts of sleep are limited to the brain and cognitive function. When we are awake, neurons in the brain produce adenosine, an additive of the cells' energy. The compiling of adenosine in the brain is one component that conducts our way of feeling or being tired. (Why Do We Sleep, Anyway? | Healthy Sleep, 2007).

This is when we tend to reach for that excessively large cup of coffee, because caffeine has the ability to block adenosine in the brain or cognitive space. This is, however, a bit counterproductive because you will eventually become immune to these caffeinated substances, and they will no longer help you keep your eyes open. So, enabling yourself to use caffeine as a means to feel less tired is not always a very good idea. Especially considering its various health adversities and the impacts too little sleep has on the rest of your aura and energy. The only truly effective way to combat adenosine or tiredness is to sleep. It is as simple as that. Surely, there are various influences that can make you feel a more constant need to sleep. This is why it is so important to be aware of what we consume or invite into our space.

Sleep also keeps our mind, body, and spirit from running into potential dangers when we are exhausted. Whenever our energy is low and our auras exhausted, we can be vulnerable to many potential dangers. Another interesting theory regarding sleep was developed quite early on. It suggested that inactivity during nighttime is a survival method for many entities to keep them out of reach of potential dangers when they are especially vulnerable.

For example, an animal capable of sleeping in a safe place and remaining completely still and undetectable, out of the peripheral sites of predators, had a better chance at survival than those who were active at night (Why Do We Sleep, Anyway? | Healthy Sleep, 2007). This survival strategy is what we now, in modern life, consider sleep. It keeps us out of trouble and out of harm's way while restoring our energy and creating balance in our various layers or bodies.

Our health is a direct reflection of the state of our aura or biofield. If our physical bodies are having a hard time, then it is most likely that our auras are suffering, too. Our physical health says a lot about our mental and spiritual being. Our physical health is also an exposure tool that highlights any shortcomings regarding our environments and their surrounding influences. That is why it is easy to tell if someone has physical health problems by glancing at their aura and taking their external environment into consideration, as well. The entire concept of nourishment is based around the idea that living beings consume food in order to stimulate growth and the growth of replacement tissue. The physical body draws out the nutrients from the object of consumption to feed itself.

Nutrition and sleep go hand in hand when it comes to overall wellness and our experiences here on Earth. We do, somehow, have more control over what we eat, and lately, there has been a huge surge in the healthy/whole foods market. To some, food can be a very challenging aspect of their life. Although there is an increasing popularity in organic and whole foods, extremely unhealthy food also sees successes on the daily. This is due to various marketing tools and the overall appeal of "fast food". In this book, there will be no preaching about avoiding fast foods and only eating a bowl of kale for every meal. Instead, a reasonable approach that considers the modern lifestyle and its appeals will be analyzed. One can simply use this chapter as a guide, just like the rest of the book.

When it comes to a balanced, nutritional approach, we have to look at it as a whole. This means we have to consider our body, mind, and spirit. Educating ourselves on nutrition can be a very concise way to incorporate it into our overall vitality and wellness. We are each unique with unique energy and a unique aura, so we have to approach nutrition with this in mind. Creating a healthy physical body can lead to various health benefits for all layers or bodies that exude within and without us.

It is also extremely important to honor our bodies and the progress we have made. By using nutrition, we have the ability to empower ourselves to take full ownership of our energy. Nutrition also helps us build immunity or strength towards certain things. This can, in turn, protect us from negative energy or the surrounding influences that enable or encourage weak or disabled energy and penetrate the vulnerable.

Nutrition and overall health are directly linked to each other. It is proven that 75 percent of the physical body's immune system is based in the digestive system. That is why it is important to pay attention to what kind of food we allow to travel through our digestive tracts.

For example, multi-colored vegetables and low-glycemic fruits are rich in plant chemicals, or phytonutrients, and can easily help the physical body fight off infections and boost the immune system. Vegetables and fruits are a key factor in every balanced lifestyle, and they are somewhat important to consume daily; every nutritionist would agree with this. We need to feed our bodies good sources of energy in order to create good energy within ourselves.

Vitamin C is another example that is known to boost immunity and help our physical bodies fight off infection. It is also a good source of energy and can help us maintain a good balance that will enable us to remain healthy in all aspects of life. When we receive good sources of energy from our food, we enable certain vibrations to be released, improving our moods, sleeping patterns, digestive health, and the way we move physically and mentally. Food is not only beneficial to our physical health but also to our mental health.

The neurotransmitter serotonin helps us regulate our sleep patterns, control our appetite, it influences our moods, and it signals the pain transmitters in our bodies. It is also produced in our gastrointestinal tract which is lined with millions of nerves and cells that help us absorb and digest food. It also, surprisingly, influences our moods and mental well-being. These functioning neurons and neurotransmitters are produced and influenced by the number of good bacteria that are present in the physical body.

Not only does good bacteria (which sounds conflicting) limit inflammation, but it also combats bad bacteria. Bad bacteria release certain toxins in the body that can cause a whole array of problems, including negativity in your aura and energy. They also act as guides to help transfer nutrients from your stomach to your brain, and when this transportation becomes imbalanced, it can disrupt your mental and emotional flow (Selhub, 2020).

Traditional diets like the Mediterranean diet and the Japanese diet are made up of organic or whole foods and rarely contain any sugar or other ingredients that could cause a build-up of toxins in the body. A study that compared this sort of lifestyle with a modern western one concluded that the people who ate more organically experienced a lower risk of depression and mental disturbances.

Because these diets hold more nutritional value, like vegetables, fruits, unprocessed meats and grains, and leaner forms of dairy, and because western dietary patterns were mostly made up of refined/hidden sugars and over-processed foods, those who followed a more traditional diet were "happier" in general (Selhub, 2020).

There are various aspects of nutritional wellness that have the possibility to affect our energy directly. This is because food is also an entity that generates energy and vibrations. However, it is important for us to eat in order to "fuel" our bodies firstly. It is not wrong to eat something unhealthy or sugary from time to time because, let's face it, it is needed to give us a dopamine surge every now and then. But this has to occur in moderation. When we eat too much of this or even eat it too often, it can become overwhelming and cause clutter in our auras, as well as a depletion in our energy levels. Bad gut bacteria, which usually comes from toxins released from unhealthy foods, can cause inflammation. This also has a very big influence on our energy levels and moods.

So, let us take a look at nutrition and sleep frame by frame or layer by layer. When we eat bad foods or follow a bad diet, it can lead to various immune deficiencies and a build-up of bad bacteria in our stomachs, which means that our bodies will most likely be ingesting toxins instead of nutrients. When this happens, we will almost certainly experience low energy levels and bad moods, which can cause emotional fatigue and stress. Stress and anxiety can spiral into sleeplessness or too much sleep, leaving our bodies in a constant need for relief or sustenance.

Nutrition also influences our self-esteem, because a bad diet and unusual sleeping patterns can cause weight gain, acne, depression, and other surrounding influences that are cause for negativity. As we know by now, the energy we consume and the energy we emit out to the universe is a direct reflection of our auras and authentic selves.

To conclude this chapter, it is important to take away from this that you cannot protect or own your energy when you are not nourishing and protecting your physical body, too. When you start listening to your physical body after feeding it, you will notice changes immediately and in the long run. When we start eating a cleaner diet, there is no need to have an extreme or rapid approach to it.

Get into the habit gradually in order to avoid the detox effect that rapid diet change can have on your energy. When a cleaner diet is followed, along with a healthy sleeping pattern, it can reduce toxic energy and negativity surrounding your aura. Sometimes, it is important to protect your energy by taking responsibility for your own bad dietary or physical health decisions.

Now that we have discussed nutrition and sleep, it is important to take a glance at the relationships you keep that also influence your aura. In the previous chapter, we discussed the concept of energy vampires. Though, not everyone in our lives are necessarily energy vampires. Sometimes the person or entity comes across as draining or incompatible because of our own demise or simply because their vibrations are not synching well with ours that day or during that specific time. There is a way to distinguish between something or someone who is a completely destructive entity towards your energy and someone or something who is just not vibing with you at that moment.

In order to establish what is going on, we must take a moment to reflect. This can be done on the spot by identifying and analyzing your surroundings and feelings, or it can be done through a ritualistic form of reflection like meditation, smudging, or other cleansing techniques that are relevant to you and your unique aura. If you sense that something might be wrong with you or your own energy, then it might be from your end. Perhaps if you encounter that being's energy on another day, then it might have a different effect on you. If you still feel like you are in a funk whenever you are near them, then it might be time to rethink this relationship or bond.

There are various signifiers that can show whether your energy is compatible with someone else's or not. When you are in the same space as this person and you notice yourself feeling more agitated than relaxed, then it might be a sign that they are emitting vibrations that do not mesh well with yours, or their actions simply do not sit well with your energy.

Another signifier is emotional depth. If you find yourself always having meaningless conversations with this person, or you feel like your conversations or exchanges are insignificant, then your energies might be incompatible, and you could be better off separate. If you are constantly misunderstood by that person, whether it is during a verbal exchange or an alternate situation you find yourself in, it can become quite challenging to share or create a meaningful bond. Relationships of any sort have to involve mutual exchange. Whether it is emotional currency or just a sense of presence, this can hold a significant amount of meaning.

When one or the other is constantly the center around which this relationship evolves, then it is not balanced, and, therefore, not something that can be deemed as a healthy relationship. The last thing to reflect on is whether you can be yourself. If you constantly feel like you have to change yourself or adjust your energy to be around them, then that might be a sign of incompatibility.

Whether it is based on nutrition, sleep, or relationships, the way safe living is practiced and positive vibes are generated will always vary from entity to entity. You are a unique being who comes with its own set of growth and wellness demands that are always important to consider. These three factors mentioned above (health, sleep, relationships) can either help you in life as a source of joy and comfort and a chance to rejuvenate, or it can become another blockage in your aura preventing you from living the wonderful life you deserve. It all depends on you, and you are extremely capable.

❧ 9 ❧

ENERGETIC DEFENSE

A s we learned in previous chapters throughout this book, it has become quite clear that in this modern life, we have removed ourselves too far from the things that actually matter as a means of comfort or survival. Our lives require most of us to work constantly, and when we are not working constantly, we are constantly thinking of working. Our personal lives can also become a demanding aspect of our modern lives to maintain.

We all continuously fill our energies and our bodies with toxins that enable us to keep up with this extremely exhausting and demanding lifestyle. That is exactly when our auras tend to weaken, and we become less capable to protect ourselves from toxic energy, energy pathogens, energy vampires, and other negative influences. Luckily, there are a few ways that we can defend our energies from these unfavorable surroundings and vibes.

One thing to take into consideration is our surrounding influences. They can cause us to lose sight of the true authentic versions of ourselves and also make us vulnerable to various pathogens because we do not keep our perspective clear. The first defense we have to consider is remaining vigilant and not becoming ignorant. Some might believe that ignorance is bliss, and, yes, it is always an easier option to ignore what is happening, but that gives negative energy the opportunity to manifest and grow. Taking control or ownership of our energy requires us to be aware of situations or things that pose a threat to our auras. When we recharge or revitalize the aura with vital nutrients and vibrations or energy, it will be able to ward off negative energy that comes from various negative energies. Negative energy does not discriminate, and it has the power to take over anyone's well-being.

Another defense that works quite well in our favor is intellect. When we stimulate the aura with intellectual vibrations, we disable any entities to influence us against our will or knowledge. This is also a strategic way to defend ourselves against the ignorance that usually clouds our judgment and enables negativity to latch onto our energy. This intellect enables us to argue or reason with someone who might be a negative entity wishing to cause damage or inflict certain emotional pain upon us. Intellect also opens certain channels that enable us to think for ourselves and become more in tune with what our aura is trying to tell us. It will also help us stimulate the parts of ourselves that are mentally struggling with judgment and empower us to come up with sustainable solutions. Intellect, when used as a defense mechanism, can and will deflect negativity away from the aura and back at the entity who has chosen to produce it.

Sometimes when we encounter negativity, we tend to withdraw ourselves from the situation. Withdrawal can be an effective way to deal with negative energy, but it can also be a little bit self-destructive if it is not handled correctly. When we are in situations where there is no way to counteract this negativity or even a way to reason with a negative entity, then withdrawing ourselves from the vibrational exchange that is occurring could be the best thing in order to protect our own energy. For example, when you find yourself arguing with someone, and you realize there is no way you can reason with this person, then withdrawing from the argument or situation in order to protect yourself from their negativity is a wise choice.

On the other hand, however, when you use a withdrawal tactic in every situation you encounter, it will eventually lead to ignorance, and you will never find a sustainable way to deal with negativity. We simply cannot walk away or choose to remain docile throughout every encounter with negativity that we come across. Withdrawal can also cause emotional clutter within the aura due to the fact that those emotions or negative vibrations have no way out. It can often lead to us losing certain people in our lives simply because we chose to sew ourselves shut instead of creating an opportunity for change. This form of disconnect often leads to other damaging defense mechanisms. However, it is important to remember that whatever we keep locked up inside will submerge eventually.

In contrast with withdrawal, we come across full-on defense. Creating contact with a negative energy or person can be quite effective sometimes if it is dealt with accordingly. Sometimes we have to address the situation head-on. It does not necessarily have to end up combatively, but creating a safe space and regulated way for that negativity to come out and face the music can be a productive defense method. For example, if you can sense negativity from someone standing across the room, you can confront them about it or simply ask them about it. Hopefully, it turns into a meaningful conversation where various aspects can be addressed. Giving that negativity the room or ability to be released can cause some sort of expenditure for whichever entity that was harboring it.

Sometimes, there just has to be a sense of relief attached to releasing a negative thought or vibration. When it exits the aura it can be resolved or even disintegrate completely. This is why tension release, or the release of negativity, is always so highly emphasized in various healing practices. When it is pursued with transparency and honesty, confrontation regarding negativity can be a progressive way to deflect it away from your aura.

There can be no possible attempt at peace within yourself and your aura if you do not practice selective defense mechanisms. There are certain negative entities or specific aspects of negative energy that just simply needs to be left alone. We cannot always get involved or address everything that comes our way. Sometimes it is better to deflect negativity away by selecting which aspects are worth dealing with and which are not. Selective defense also helps us prioritize the things that are affecting our energy. Usually, when it is something that we have no control over, or if it is something within ourselves that we cannot control, the best way to deal with it is to carefully pick the parts of it that can be dealt with, and then proceed in that order. One does not necessarily ignore negativity, but by prioritization, you can learn which is more crucial to deal with or abolish first.

For example, if we drink too much, we can get a hangover. The hangover is not necessarily the root of the problem, and neither is the alcohol. The fact that the alcohol acts as a diuretic and dehydrates us is the actual problem. So, by using selective defense, we will combat the dehydration aspect of it first in order to deal with the problem as a whole. Our auras can benefit from the same approach. If we draw out the part that needs attention the most and address it first, it can make the rest of the situation easier to convert to positivity or to deflect the negativity.

A clean aura, as we previously discussed, is a strong aura. When we cleanse our energy, we strengthen it by getting rid of impurities and enabling certain parts of ourselves to heal and replenish. Aura or energy cleansing can involve a variety of different things which make us more resilient towards certain attacks on our energy. Surely, offense is the best defense, but in this case, we are becoming more defensive by combating impurities before they even have the opportunity to manifest.

When your energy is cleansed, revitalized, and vibrant, it can be the best defense there is. This is because a healthy aura will deflect any negative energy that dares to come its way. Aura baths can cleanse our auras, as well as our physical bodies. Also, essential oils and herbs can have healing properties that repair previous abrasions that might still be vulnerable. They also cleanse us from the outside in.

Smudging with sage can cleanse our aura and the physical space we take up and create a resilient energy that will conjure up the strength to protect us against various negative pathogens. When the space is cleansed, it makes it nearly impossible for negative energy to latch on. Another important thing that defends our auras from negativity is spending time in nature. Not only do our physical bodies receive nutrients like Vitamin D from the sun, but our mental and emotional bodies are nourished with light and tranquility, which leaves us confident and content in dealing with negativity.

The final emphasis on aura cleansing is using positive affirmations. If we feed our thoughts positive assertions, it will nourish our auras and energy with positivity. Whether you feed it to yourself verbally or through another medium, this form of positivity that you send to your own energy can strengthen the bond you have with yourself. Also, as we previously learned, whatever we put out into the universe has a way to come back to us. Therefore, if we manifest positive energy unto ourselves, it will make it extremely hard for negative energy to penetrate our auras.

It might not seem possible for some of us, but sometimes creating space between ourselves and other entities can be an admirable and dignified method of defense. Some argue that other problems may come from creating space. However, ultimately space, just like sleep, can give our energy a chance to recuperate and rebuild. It can also open up an opportunity for reflection, because space also gives us time to rethink our actions or thoughts. Creating distance can avoid negativity. Even though we should never neglect any signs of energy coming our way, some distance might give us an opportunity to evaluate this energy and its possible outcomes before it enters our auras or physical space.

Sometimes distance creates clarity; what we are able to comprehend up close is not always the same as what we comprehend through distance. We are all familiar with the term "absence makes the heart grow fonder". This is somewhat relevant to our experiences with other energy forces. Distance can cause the negativity to become more thinly spread until it ultimately regenerates itself into positive energy. For example, when we separate ourselves from a loved one after an argument, we can reflect on our own issues and realize where our own faults were. That way, when we encounter them again, we will have the opportunity to make amends.

The final defense mechanism we will be discussing is a way to use empathy against negativity. This is most useful when we tend to react negatively towards an entity, because it is launching an attack on our own energy. This is especially useful when dealing with conflict. When we understand or anticipate where an entity's negativity stems from, we can find a way to resolve it before it ends up contaminating our own energy.

Empathy involves some internalizing of others' negativity, but ultimately it reflects this back onto them as a strategic way for them to realize they are sending out low vibrations. When we react with compassion towards negativity, it can often create an opportunity for this negative force to recalculate and reflect. We deflect negativity with empathy by refusing to let negativity enter our auric space and turn us into negative entities. Simply put, it is a lot like fighting hate with love.

It is always our responsibility to fill our auras with healthy, positive, and loving vibrations in order to strengthen it and prevent negative energy from chewing away until it has struck our core. These defenses will ultimately enable us to strengthen our mental, physical, and spiritual existence to the point where it is almost impossible for negative energy to impact us in any way.

Defenses are not a way to enter a combative act in order to protect yourself, but merely an approach that aids in prevention instead of reaction. We are all unique beings, and it is important to approach every person we encounter with love, light, and warmth. In these modern times, it is easier to keep your guard up, because that is how we make ourselves feel safe. But safety will hold us back, and our spirits are here to explore, discover, and enlighten one another. We need to be open, but vigilant. That is how we can own and protect our energy at the same time.

❧ 10 ❧

MEDITATION

A lot of people are extremely skeptical when it comes to the practice of meditation. Some feel it is a waste of time because they affiliate it with the idea of "doing nothing". That in itself is often associated with uselessness, time-wasting, and ineffectiveness. However, sometimes doing nothing can save you time and make you do more useful things or act in more useful ways. In other words, it has been proven to be quite an effective activity.

It is not always an easy task, and not everyone gets it right straight away. Our brains are extremely complex organs. Even though the brain is a big part of our sense of authentic self, it can still be quite daunting and difficult to get our minds to become completely clear and still. It can be used for various reasons, and sometimes you do not even have to take too much time out of your day to complete an exercise. You can even do it while sitting at your desk, and that is why it is such a convenient way to cleanse, brighten, and protect your aura.

Part of taking ownership and learning to protect your energy is learning how to ease your mind and spirit. This is also a form of cleansing and can be extremely beneficial. It is quite easy to create a habit out of meditation and mindful breathing once you become more comfortable with the practice and execution.

To put it simply, meditation can be whatever you make of it. It can be a way of focusing your attention on one thing only, like mindful meditation. When we meditate mindfully, we focus on one thing and one thing only. Whenever our mind or attention shifts to something else, we teach it how to divert back. This enables us or teaches us how to keep our minds from wandering. This sort of meditation can also improve our ability to focus or concentrate, which is beneficial in real-life scenarios, too.

Open-monitoring meditation is the exact opposite and enables your mind to focus on everything that is happening around it, without reacting to it. When we meditate, our minds do not process information at the same speed that it usually does. The frontal lobe which is responsible for most of our alertness switches off, which causes a calming sensation to spread. Being able to give this part of the brain a break now and then can act as a sort of "refresh" button.

It is said that meditation increases focus and creativity and decreases anxiety. When we meditate, we exercise our minds so they will focus on one thing (or many) at once. The more we do it, the better we become at it, like most things in life. Meditation also helps us control our anxiety, because we tend to become anxious due to our surroundings and our minds. Meditation can teach our brains to ignore certain surroundings or even senses within our bodies and only focus on one central thought or concept. On the other hand, it can teach us how to be fully aware of all these surrounding things but totally become unreactive or unresponsive towards them. Meditation helps us understand our mind, body, and spirit better by spending quality time with them.

Our creativity tends to spike whenever we start meditating. This could be because we learn how to channel certain parts of ourselves without causing any disruption in our auras. When we are fully awake, (not meditating or asleep), our thoughts tend to rush through our minds quite quickly. Thus, whenever we think of something creative, it just zooms past, and we forget about it. Meditation teaches us to slow things down and become more in-tune with our minds and spirits. It can also enable us to control our emotions a bit better.

Meditating helps us get rid of the things that cause clutter in our minds and auras. When we declutter, any negativity can be recycled into positivity or completely deviated away from us. It is also believed that meditation improves our memory because of its ability to shift our focus to one thing, or it enables us to ignore a whole conglomerate of things that are happening around us.

Breathing gives the body the oxygen it needs to function. It is arguably the most important part of our existence, because it keeps our physical bodies alive. It is a natural process that happens on its own, and we rarely give it the credit or the acknowledgment that it deserves. This could be because we never pay attention to it unless we run out of it while walking up and down the stairs every now and then. Breathing is not only linked to our physical bodies but also our spiritual and mental bodies.

In Hindu and Yogi cultures and subcultures, breathing has always been a very significant act. People always think of yoga as a physical movement exercise, when in actuality it is also fundamentally based on breathing. Every single move that is incorporated into yoga has a certain breathing method attached to it. In yoga, these breathing methods or patterns teach you how to control your breath physically in order to enhance and use it mindfully and spiritually. It is safe to say we do not only breathe to keep our physical bodies alive, but also our mental and spiritual bodies.

Buddhism also incorporated mindful breathing into their traditions. Ānāpānasati Sutta, a very relevant Buddhist text, mentions mindful breathing along with many other meditative insights and other scripts about meditation. It is also important to remember that breathing in and out is not just something we do to obtain and release oxygen from our physical bodies. When we inhale and exhale, it is also an exchange of energy (Mindful Exercises, n.d.). We basically breathe in our surroundings and their energy and exhale our energy out onto the world. There are various ways in which breathing is linked to energy, but the most important take from this should be that mindful breathing can be extremely beneficial in our efforts to gain control over our energy and in our attempts to protect ourselves.

There are many different breathing exercises you can try, such as different pranayama techniques taught by yogis that go hand in hand with different movements and steps. Although these can be extremely powerful and beneficial, it does not necessarily have to be that intricate. Mindful breathing can be a very simple and gracious task for all of us. The main focus of mindful breathing should only be on the breathing; do not worry about the rest.

Step 1: Step into a comfortable position. You can either sit or lie down - whichever one suits you best. The only thing to remember here is to keep your back straight and the rest of your body still and relaxed.

Step 2: Relax completely without losing that straightness in your back, and try to become completely grounded in the space that you are currently occupying. You can do this by becoming aware of what you are physically feeling against your body - the temperature, the sensations - whichever aspects that you can identify in order to make you feel grounded.

Step 3: Focus on the rhythm or positioning of your breath, but be careful not to try and change it or control it just yet. All you have to do is observe how it moves and when it is inhaling or exhaling. Allow any changes that might occur during your natural breathing pattern, and just roll with it. Try to remain completely focused on each and every breath. You will notice a pause between exhaling and inhaling; you should also take those small intervals into consideration.

That is all it takes to practice mindful breathing. Just ground yourself in a comfortable and relaxed position, and focus completely on your breathing without trying to control its natural flow or patterns. It can be done anywhere and at any time. Mindful breathing can exist on its own and is not just a part of full-blown yoga or meditation practices. You can practice this in any setting, which also makes it extremely convenient because we can even incorporate it into our extremely busy routines.

Mindful breathing has a whole cluster of benefits that comes with it. Just like meditation and other practices, it can be an instant way to reduce stress. This is mainly because it can induce calming responses in the body instead of the usual frantic breathing patterns, which we barely recognize within ourselves. It reduces the number of stress hormones we release into our bodies which is beneficial to all aspects of the aura as well. We all know by now how badly stress can affect our energy.

When we practice mindful breathing, whether it is for three minutes or three hours, it can help us become grounded in our current environment. As we previously mentioned regarding the beneficial aspects of meditation, when we become grounded and aware of our surrounding influences, we can learn to disassociate from it or acknowledge it and become non-reactive towards it. This can cause a reduction in our levels of anxiety and enable us to gain some control over our current state of mind. It also helps to control the chemicals our bodies send to our brain. This is a complicated and scientific concept, but in simple terms, it basically contributes to the cellular growth and connections between our bodies and our brains. It is also linked to better sleeping patterns, because our mental state is extremely tied into them. Mindful breathing soothes the body and mind, which simply leads to more concise sleeping patterns (Mindful Exercises, n.d.).

As we discussed previously, there are copious amounts of benefits within the concept of mindful breathing, and it is nearly impossible to discuss each and every one of them in this book. Mindful breathing can pretty much be adopted into your everyday lifestyle extremely easily and be a useful quick fix when you cannot fit in a meditation ritual.

Meditation can help us find the strength we need to protect our energy. It gives us a moment to gather up all our energy and use it mindfully to better ourselves. We are unique beings who often forget that we all deal with things differently. Sometimes we might feel like we are losing our grip a bit, and we might stumble into a case of low energy and vibration. We often feel the need to reconnect with ourselves and remember who we are and how capable and powerful we can be. In order to improve the strength of our energy, we can do the following exercise:

Step 1: Focus on your mindful breathing. Sit in a comfortable position with your back straight. Breathe in and out comfortably and make sure your breathing patterns are natural and deep.

Step 2: Close your eyes. Now start to think of a difficult situation that you are currently in or might find yourself in later. Focus on your breathing, and take note of any changes. If you start to breathe heavily when this thought process starts, then that is how you know it might be a significant part of your life.

Step 3: Now that you are envisioning this situation and focusing on your breathing, try to pinpoint any fears or anxieties that this situation is instilling upon you. Whether it is a physical pain or unwellness, or an emotional trigger does not matter; just try to identify those pain points.

Please keep in mind that this situation or scenario that you are conjuring up can be anything that is affecting you, big or small. For example, it can be a confrontational conversation that needs to occur between you and someone else or a painful procedure that you have to endure.

Step 4: Instead of trying to think of all the possible outcomes that this situation or event could have, try to shift your attention to the strongest version of yourself. Instead, imagine yourself being the strongest version of yourself, and then envision what that version of you would do in such a situation. Envision yourself handling the situation kindly, confidently, patiently, cohesively, and accordingly.

Step 5: As you are envisioning yourself handling the situation this way, try to think of adjectives that you would like to be associated with. After you have envisioned yourself in that way, start to recognize those aspects within you. For example, if you want to be associated with strength, think of a certain strength you have within you, whether it is the strength to carry on through tough times or the strength to carry others emotionally. Just make sure you identify and highlight those aspects internally.

Step 6: Allow yourself to feel strong, confident, or resilient. When you start to envision yourself a certain way, then that imagery will turn into a true emotion. Try to manifest that within yourself, and allow yourself to feel the way you would like to feel during that experience.

Step 7: This step should be approached with some caution. If you do not feel like the previous positive affiliation or adjective you associated yourself with has manifested yet, then repeat step 6 until you feel like it has been incorporated properly. When that affiliation has manifested and latched onto you, try to contradict it. Now, this might seem useless, but in reality, you will lose this feeling again or some negative entity may be cause for your attention to shift. So, enabling yourself to rebuild or divert this attention back to the positive will require some training, but if you repeat it constantly, you will be able to do it comfortably.

Step 8: Reconnect with that positive affiliation within yourself once again, and associate yourself with the positivity that you want to feel. Repeating those positive affirmations to yourself or replaying that positive vision in your mind will eventually enable you to make it into your reality. By doing this, you will ensure that those positive affiliations and strengths manifest within you. You can carry on with one capability, repeating it multiple times. You can also practice this by using different scenarios, situations, or events. This is a very intuitive way to prepare yourself for a whole variety of experiences. Just remember to breathe and focus on your triggers.

This meditation exercise can be done whenever and wherever. Just make sure you remain focused throughout the process so that your energy does not become stuck on one perspective. Also keep in mind that there are hundreds of meditative exercises you can practice, so it is always possible to switch it up every now and then. If you incorporate meditation into your routine and turn it into a ritual or a habit, you will surely see yourself grow and realize how it benefits your energy all around. Meditation is one of the most effective ways to protect and own our energy.

CONCLUSION

Remember to think of your energy as a natural entity, because you are physically a natural entity, as well. When you or your aura receives the correct nutrition, nourishment, and light, you will grow stronger and more resilient each and every day. When you starve, butcher, or neglect yourself, you open yourself up to negative energy like toxic energy, pathogens, and many other influences that can defeat your energy. Also, you will deteriorate or disable your growth unless you manage to rescue yourself or find solitude amongst other things. You need love, joy, and light in order to grow into the beautiful and majestic life force that you are, so allow it to enter your aura. Take extreme care of your body, mind, and spirit, and you will be able to maintain a vibrant and resilient aura.

We know that an accumulation of toxic energy can cause clutter and an overwhelming sense of pressure on our auras, which exponentially overwhelms our whole existence and life force. This can have a very damaging effect on our lives, because our minds and our physical bodies can crumble under this falling tower of energy. The purpose of this book was to enable you to protect yourself and your energy and prevent this from happening, because you deserve a magnificent and enriched life.

We did discuss some very heavy or negative things during this journey, but it is important to familiarize yourself with them in order to protect your energy. This was a method to keep you from feeling ambushed or becoming a victim of randomized energy attacks. As stated in the second chapter, this book is meant to be a guiding light through your journey to the road of empowerment and learning how to protect your energy. You are able when you are willing, and you are protected when you are wise.

There are so many possible ways for things like energy vampires to enter our space and use our energy for their own gain. Whether they are able to recognize their abuse or not, it is impossible for us to even know what their intentions are and can be. Because we are entities filled with love and light, it is not always possible for us to identify these entities because we are unable to pass judgment right away. It can be extremely challenging to remain vigilant around these types of beings because of their seductive ways and even their sense of allure.

However, if we remain self-assured in our capabilities to deflect their actions, we will be able to protect our energy. When we own our energy, we conjure up capabilities that we never knew we had, and we can even surprise ourselves with how much strength and resilience we contain within ourselves. It can be hard sometimes to remain a source of light in a seemingly dark world. However, you are a courageous being with a very unique aura that is there to guide and protect you through all your discouragements, even those pesky energy vampires.

Remember that when we look at an unhealthy aura, it can be a sign that the entity and that aura surrounding it are in trouble. Auras that have been infected by an energy pathogen become easier and easier to distinguish, and you will be able to identify them quickly over time. You now understand that they lose the vibrancy of their aura, and this can cause dull and dark color variations. The shape of their aura, which should ideally be an egg, will appear patchy or jagged. It can also have bulges and dents in it. Simply put, if it does not look right, then it probably is not alright. You will start recognizing these signifiers in your own or in others' auras, but now you will know how to proceed and that you have to pay attention to it as soon as possible. Energy does not lie, and neither does one's aura.

During these challenging modern times, it can become quite hard to stay in tune with ourselves and maintain a well-balanced life. Reaching out to healers and trying out various rituals can help us restore balance in our lives and assist us in maintaining it, as well. In a world where gym memberships, plastic surgery, crash diets, and various other vanities are prioritized over inner beauty, it is important to always focus inwards first.

Your physical body is the vessel that you travel this earth with. Heal it, protect it, and nourish it, and eventually, it will do the same for your mind and your spirit. When we struggle to find beauty in the world or even within ourselves, we should always turn to nature. One must always remember the healing and clarity nature can bring us. We come from it; therefore, we must use it to nourish our body, mind, and spirit as often as we possibly can.

When you happen to feel a bit overwhelmed or hopeless, do not perceive this as a call for immediate action unless you think it is extremely serious or an extremely negative energy that is busy entering your aura. Allow yourself to feel things, whether they are good or bad. This is what makes us human, and it is okay to be human as far as we know. The idea is just to be the best person that we possibly can be.

Keep in mind that every single living being, especially the ones on planet Earth, is capable of healing itself. Healers have used energy fields for thousands of years in order to establish certain diagnoses. Auric or biofield healing therapies were developed early on and used as identifiers and healing methods for pain, cell rejuvenation, immune boosting, and, of course, spiritual healing. You can, will, and are capable of healing yourself and even finding healing and clarity through the help of others.

One of our weaknesses is our inability to ask for help when we cannot help ourselves. Let go of your pride, and always reach out when you start to feel like your light is dimming. The right people know you, and even if it is subconscious, they know what your aura and energy needs. If you do not have someone like that in your life or feel like you do not, there is always a way to make new connections that will welcome you into their circle. Seek and you shall find, as they say.

When we try to become the best versions of ourselves, it is important that we let go of the fact that we, as humans, are always prone to making assumptions. Assumptions are detrimental thoughts that cause more and more unnecessary issues in the world. When we let go of them, we enable ourselves to become more open to possible enlightenment. Assumptions are premeditated thoughts on something that has not been experienced, discussed, or analyzed rationally yet. When we are feeling conflicted, it is always best to let go of our preconceived notions and leave a door open for fresh and insightful thoughts and conversations.

It is our duty to fill our auras with healthful, encouraging, and loving vibrations in order to improve it and prevent negative energy from gnawing away until it has hit our core. These defenses that we have discussed throughout the book will hopefully enable you to strengthen your mental, physical, and spiritual existence to the point where it is almost impossible for negative energy to affect you. Defenses are not a way to enter a combative act in order to protect yourself, but merely an approach that aids in prevention instead of reaction.

You are a unique spirit, and it is important to approach every other spirit we encounter with love, light, and warmth. In this life, it is easier to keep your guard up, because that is what you may think safety and security should be like. But safety will hold you back, and our spirit is here to explore, discover, and enlighten others. You need to be open but vigilant. Being secure means taking ownership of your energy, and that is how you own and protect your energy simultaneously.

These concepts and theories regarding energy have been around for thousands of years, and it has been prevalent in hundreds of cultures, traditions, and religions. It is important to respect these theories and practices, not only because we benefit from them, but also because they are powerful concepts that have improved the lives of those around us. Most, if not all, of these practices have a great love and respect for the earth, and we should aim to pay the same respects to our earthly home as we do to these beliefs and practices. Not only should we respect healers, but it is our duty to support all of our fellow beings on whichever path they have chosen, whether it is our preferred road or not.

You have to take responsibility for the actions you perform on yourself, too. It is always important to be kind to yourself but also constructive. If you constantly push yourself too far in order to reach a certain goal, then you are opening yourself up to negative energy or being the negative energy in your own life. Working hard can be extremely rewarding, but it can also be just as draining. You are in complete control, and there is no need for you to push yourself until you fall to pieces. Take life as it comes, and give yourself a break every now and then. You will be amazed at how effective that will be in the long run.

Meditate, spend time in nature, relax regularly, and engage in activities or conversations that bring you clarity and joy. You might think that you are moving towards a successful life, but if you are too hard on yourself, you will burn out before you even get there. Becoming a well-balanced entity and maintaining powerful energy is often a challenging journey as we already know. That is why you should remember to avoid depriving yourself of the things that make you truly love life. Live and let live.

You are now at the end of this book and fully equipped to start taking ownership of your energy and protecting it. If you have already started your journey and used this book, then the same goes for you. YOU are a unique aura that emits unique energy onto the universe and, throughout your life, you will encounter many experiences that will bring you light, joy, love, and gratification. In contrast, you will experience many hardships - times where it will be hard for you to remain a positive entity. However, you will succeed, because you now have ownership and protection over your energy.

It is not an easy journey; the road can sometimes be filled with many obstacles. But you have made it this far for a reason, and you are a capable, strong, and radiant being that can withstand any storm that comes your way. Remember to be the light source for others when they need it, but not to drown yourself in your efforts. Remember to love those who need it, and even those you think do not. Remember to celebrate your accomplishments and clap for others when they win.

But most importantly, remember that you are a unique life force, and you have the capability to live a fulfilled life. You will feel these forces come back to you in abundance; just keep on spreading those positive vibes.

REFERENCES

American School of Hypnosis. (2015, November 19). 7 Types of Energy Vampires and How-To Slay Them [Video]. YouTube. https://www.youtube.com/watch?v=lCc5wucgsys

Brain waves and meditation. (2010, March 31). ScienceDaily; The Norwegian University of Science and Technology (NTNU). https://www.sciencedaily.com/releases/2010/03/100319210631.htm

Brazier, Y. (2017, December 21). How does acupuncture work? Medical News Today. https://www.medicalnewstoday.com/articles/156488#what%20to%20expect

Buchowski-Kurus, M. (n.d.). Dark Spirit Vs. Divine Light. AYU-OK Holistic Healing. Retrieved June 29, 2020, from https://www.ayuok.com/spirit-dark-light

Carroll, R. T. (2015, December 17). Energy (New Age). The Skeptic's Dictionary. http://skepdic.com/energy.html

Carroll, R. T. (2015, December 17). Energy (New Age). The Skeptic's Dictionary. http://skepdic.com/energy.html

Henshaw, S. (2018, July 8). How To Avoid Being Drained By Energy Vampires. Psych Central; Psych Central. https://psychcentral.com/blog/how-to-avoid-being-drained-by-energy-vampires/

Hive, T. W. (2019, October 24). 9 objects that spread negative energy around the house. Homify.In. https://www.homify.in/ideabooks/4448115/9-objects-that-spread-negative-energy-around-the-house

How the Biofield Communicates. (n.d.). The Bioenergy Balancing Center; The Bioenergy Balancing Center. Retrieved June 26, 2020, fromhttps://balancingcenter.com/how-the-biofield-communicates/

Martin, B. Y. (2008, May 13). The Aura and Health. Spiritual Arts Institute. https://spiritualarts.org/blog/change-your-aura/the-aura-and-health/

Mindful Exercises. (n.d.). Mindful Exercises. Retrieved July 5, 2020, from https://mindfulnessexercises.com/6-mindful-breathing-exercises/

Newman, T. (2017, September 6). Everything you need to know about reiki. Medical News Today. https://www.medicalnewstoday.com/articles/308772#health-benefits

Northrup, C. (2018). Dodging Energy Vampires: An Empath's Guide to Evading Relationships That Drain You and Restoring Your Health and Powe (1st ed., Vol. 1, pp. 1–5). Hay House Inc.

Price, C. (2020, April 15). Trapped - the secret ways social media is built to be addictive (and what you can do to fight back). BBC Science Focus Magazine. https://www.sciencefocus.com/future-technology/trapped-the-secret-ways-social-media-is-built-to-be-addictive-and-what-you-can-do-to-fight-back/

Ranzani, O. T., Milà, C., Kulkarni, B., Kinra, S., & Tonne, C. (2020). Association of Ambient and Household Air Pollution With Bone Mineral Content Among Adults in Peri-urban South India. JAMA Network Open, 3(1), e1918504. https://doi.org/10.1001/jamanetworkopen.2019.18504

S. (2018, August 14). The Proven Science Behind Biofield Healing. Biofield Healing Institute®. https://biofieldhealinginstitute.com/proven-science-behind-biofield-healing/

Selhub, E. (2020, March 31). Nutritional psychiatry: Your brain on food. Harvard Health Blog. https://www.health.harvard.edu/blog/nutritional-psychiatry-your-brain-on-food-201511168626

Svirinskaya, A. (2019). Own your energy: develop immunity to toxic energy and preserve your authentic life force (1st ed.). Hay House.

Svirinskaya, A. (n.d.). Alla Svirinskaya - energy healing. www.AllaSvirinskaya.Com. Retrieved June 25, 2020, from http://www.allasvirinskaya.com/

Tips to help boost immunity. (2020, May 1). Holistic Nutrition. https://www.holisticnutrition.co.uk/tips-to-help-boost-immunity/

Why Do We Sleep, Anyway? | Healthy Sleep. (2007, December 18). Division of Sleep Medicine at Harvard Medical School. http://healthysleep-.med.harvard.edu/healthy/matters/benefits-of-sleep/why-do-we-sleep

Wills, B. (2019, March 18). How to Take a Holistic Approach to Problem Solving. Ameritech College of Healthcare. https://www.ameritech.edu/blog/6-ways-approach-problems-holistically/

YOUR FEEDBACK IS VALUED

We would like to be so bold as to ask for an act of kindness from you. If you read and enjoyed our book/s, would you please consider leaving an honest review on Amazon or audible? As an independent publishing group, your feedback means the absolute world to us. We read every single review we receive and would love to hear your thoughts, as each piece of feedback helps us serve you better. Your feedback may also impact others across the globe, helping them discover powerful knowledge they can implement in their lives to give them hope and self-empowerment. Wishing you empowerment, courage, and wisdom on your journey.

If you have read or listened to any of our books and would be so kind as to review them, you can do so by clicking the 'learn more' tab under the book's picture on our website:

https://ascendingvibrations.net/books

Why not join our Facebook community and discuss your spiritual path with like-minded seekers?

We would love to hear from you!

Go here to join the 'Ascending Vibrations' community:
bit.ly/ascendingvibrations

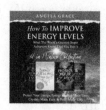

CLAIM YOUR *BONUS* AUDIOBOOK

If you love listening to audio books on-the-go, I have great news for you. You can download the 13 hour + audiobook version of *How To Improve Energy Levels' (Energy Healing Made Easy, Crystals Made Easy, Reiki Made Easy & Protect Your Energy - 4 in 1 Collection)* for **FREE** just by signing up for a **FREE** 30-day audible trial! See below for more details!

Audible trial benefits

As an audible customer, you'll receive the below benefits with you 30-day free trial:

- Free audible copy of this book
- After the trial, you will get 1 credit each month to use on any audiobook

- Your credits automatically roll over to the next month if you don't use them
- Choose from over 400,000 titles
- Listen anywhere with the audible app across multiple devices
- Make easy, no hassle exchanges of any audiobook you don't love
- Keep your audiobooks forever, even if you cancel your membership

And much more.

Go to the links below to get started:

Go here for AUDIBLE US: bit.ly/howtoimproveenergy

Go here for AUDIBLE UK: bit.ly/howtoimproveenergyuk

Made in the USA
Monee, IL
13 March 2024

55024377R00059